THE CufflinkFORMULA™

$$C = vcd^2$$

Root values
Choices
Decisions
Judgment
Goals
Challenges
Dilemmas
Framing
Opportunities
Vision
Success

DEAD END

KEEP RIGHT

TH!NK

DO NOT ENTER

ONLY

R.I.P.

REPORT CARD

a young person's guide to decision-making

ROCKLIN JACKSON

THE CUFFLINK FORMULA™

A YOUNG PERSON'S GUIDE TO DECISION-MAKING

First Edition Copyright © 2018 by

TheCufflinkFormula@gmail.com

The Cufflink Formula

ISBN – 978-0578545288
ISBN – 0578545284
Cover Design & Concept by Rocklin Jackson
Digital Illustration Artist: Lou Jackson
Artwork Name: The Cufflink Formula TM 2019 by Rocklin Jackson
Series: 3.0 – IRJP - 2025
Email: TheCufflinkFormula@gmail.com

POWER OF YOUR PURCHASE

A portion of the proceeds made from sales
of this book will be donated to non-profit organizations
that focus on mentoring youth.

For discounts on bulk orders of 50 units or more, please contact us via email:

TheCufflinkFormula@gmail.com

Editor: Tracy Kisgen   TRKISGEN.COM

First Edition. Copyright © 2018

Next In Line Publishing Company

In Honor Of:

Frances Ann Jackson
My beautiful mother, who demonstrated love and
taught me the value of education.
– R. I. P. –

★ ★ ★

My grandchildren, whom I love and wish happy childhoods
and productive lives as adults.

Especially For:

Troubled and abused youths who unbeknownst
to themselves are on a sacred journey
of Initiation and in need of guidance.

★ ★ ★

Any person in confinement that chooses to
transform their life by courageously
footing the road less traveled.

Table of Contents

ACKNOWLEDGMENTS

I am because we are, and because we are, therefore, I am.
African Proverb

Special thanks to:

CHANCE FOR LIFE ORGANIZATION
Thomas J. Adams, President
Jessica Taylor, Executive Director

Thank You to the following people
who have served as mentors and prison volunteers:

Bishop Mbiyu Chui, Dr. Reginald Larry (R.I.P.), Mwalimu Rick Talley (R.I.P.), Mohamed Hassan (R.I.P.), Dr. Lora Bex Lempert, Dr. Paul Drauss, Gwendolyn Diane Burton, Professor Wendy Readous (R.I.P.), Anthony "Ambidwele" Carter, Brian Bush, Marcus Robinson, Nzingha Masani, Hon. Bruce U. Morrow, Attorney Susan Meinberg, Joyce Pearson, John Miggins, Steve Elturk, Tauheed Rashad, Hon. Michael Switalski, Lori Pompa, Professor Ebonie Byndon-Fields, Minister Orlando Gregory, Chef James Spence, Dr. Carl Taylor, Hon. Frank S. Szymanski, Hon. Deborah Thomas, Attorney Craig A. Daly, Attorney Jeffrey L. Edison, Attorney DeWayne R. Boyd, Professor Earl Henderson, Rev. Stephanie Fauntleroy, Maat Seba, Rev. Christian Adams, Minister Gary Hayes, Isiah Williams, Rev. Timothy Williams, Jennifer Rincones, Pastor Earlene Edwards, Pastor James Edwards, Minister Sam Burts, Paul Johnson, Keevin Ousley, Rev. Kurk Edwards, Minister Florence Piernas, Serena Sledge, Anita Adams, Rose Gorman, Michael Lauchlan, Benny White, Romain Blanquart, Billy Kidd, DPD Chaplain Kevin Earley, Sheriff Robert Dunlap, Joseph Williams, Victor Muhammad, Clementine Barfield, Hon. Heaster Wheeler, Ife Nabawi, Mother Ayo (R.I.P.), Minister Troy Muhammad, Minister Rasul Muhammad, Minister Abdul Rahman Foggie, Doris Grimsley (R.I.P.), Jeff Gerritt, Andrea Isom, Art Blackwell, Karl I. Bell, Amy Harris, Joyce Dixon, Professor Dr. Lynn Lewis, Ellery McIvor, Professor Buzz Alexander (R.I.P.), Professor Matthew Larson (Ph.D.), Professor Erin Comartin (Ph.D.), Olivia Winey, Danielle Hicks, DPD Officer E. Franklin, DPD Officer D. Maples, DPD Officer D. Harris, Valunda Watkins, Cindy Owens, Rev. & Mrs. McKeithen, Kwame Kenyetta (R.I.P.), Tamarie Willis (LLMSW), Paula & Felix Sirls, Rosalind Andrews Worthy, Keith Bennett, Lindsay Levin, Rene Gross, Keith D. Jones (LMSW), Leah Ouellet, and Stu Jackson.

ACKNOWLEDGMENTS

Special thanks to my family and friends for your love, encouragement, and support.

I am particularly grateful to my son, DeAngelo Rocklin Jackson, for being a huge part of the motivation behind my spiritual and moral transformation. I've strived to do better in order to give you better; this book is a small part of that effort. I love you and I'm proud of the good man you've become. Thank you!

Thank you to my sisters Tracey F. Jackson and Kimberly Boyd. Your love and friendships are a blessing to my spirit!

This book may never have reached its final form without the help of my brother Lou Jackson, who spent many hours preparing and arranging the material in digital format. Thank you, brother, for your wealth of knowledge and sharing your technical experience.

Thank you, one thousand times, over to Lolita S. Portwood for always being a team player. Your love and support throughout the years continues to be a blessing!

Thank you to my dear friend, Abdus-Shakur. I appreciate you always having my back and believing in the righteousness and victory of our struggle. Much love, brother!

An abundance of thanks to my brothers who I was blessed to work with in re-establishing and growing the Youth Deterrent Program (YDP) at Ryan Correctional Facility (later renamed Detroit Reentry Center). Much love and a heartfelt "Thank You!" to all my wonderful brothers!

Darryl J. Woods, Sr.	Dewayne P. Witherspoon	Brian C. Burton
Kendrick Youngblood	James Hill-El	Michael A. Tubbs
Ricardo Ferrell	Ichard Odom	Shannon L. Keys
Little E. Smith-El	Lynn McNeal	Carlton Banks
Michael Hatfield	David L. Walton	Antonio James

And a very special thank you to Jeffrey Allison, who for many years served as staff facilitator for our inspiring YDP sessions.

Thank you to my brothers in the Chance for Life Organization. Both your encouragement and critique have been helpful in many ways. My deepest gratitude with prayers for continued growth, freedom and success!

Tracy Kisgen, I appreciate you ensuring the material in this book has been presented in its best form. Thank you for doing a superb editing job.

FOREWORD

Over ten (10) years ago, I met [Everett] Rocklin Jackson at the Ryan Correctional Facility (now Detroit Reentry Center) in Detroit, MI. As the Executive Director of the Chance For Life Organization (CFL), I was charged with creating a program curriculum that dealt specifically with "Transforming" the mindset of inmates. Rocklin was chosen to participate in the long-term project and by the end of the first class, I knew he was not an ordinary "joe" and would do something great one day. And something great, he did!

He has completed the first edition of *The Cufflink Formula* which will arm young people with the knowledge and good sense to make informed choices in uncertain situations. Adolescence is the critical period between childhood and adulthood, and it is a time when youth need to develop the attitudes, values, and social skills that will move them toward successful adulthood. It is also a time when they should avoid choices that will limit their future potential. That's exactly what The Cufflink Formula is designed to do. More than mere stories, *The Cufflink Formula* is filled with an imagined sequence of events about street survival that teaches the reader how to make the best decisions for a given situation before he/she encounters it in real-life, which could possibly be detrimental. The examples of hypothetical people and predicaments are followed by the Author cleverly asking deep questions that probe profoundly into thinking before accepting ideas of friends or others as worthy of belief. This method of questioning ("*Socratic Questioning*") can be traced back 2500 years ago to Socrates and is the best-known critical thinking strategy. In his mode of questioning, he emphasizes the need in thinking for clarity and logical consistency.

In *The Cufflink Formula*, the Author creatively uses "Cufflinks" and "Handcuffs" as symbols of making good and bad choices. Graphic details are included in some of the scenarios for young people whose minds are drifting in the wrong direction. The realistic details are used to encourage open discussions about serious criminal behavior and its consequences. Current data is indicating that a number of prisons will be built to house the children of our youth if they continue this erroneous thinking. With that in mind, what is the best choice you can make right now? READ THIS BOOK! Not only will you be making an investment in your own self-development, but you will also be investing in the future of your children and grandchildren. While written primarily to help young people, this comprehensive book is essential reading for anyone who wants to increase their ability to make good decisions. Because young people are newcomers on the path of social, moral and spiritual development, they need guides to help them along the way. *The Cufflink Formula* will guide them through their everyday choices and experiences and give them the skills necessary to become responsible adults. If you need to find the courage and strength to make good decisions and the confidence to stay the course, I strongly recommend to everyone to read this book and share it with the young people in your life.

Although, he has been confined in prison for the past 32 years, [Everett] Rocklin Jackson managed to raise his own son using these same principles. His son is now a successful business owner and devotes his time to helping those who have a parent that is incarcerated.

Jessica Taylor
Executive Director
Chance For Life Organization
Southfield, MI

"The choices you make today are the down-payment on your future."

INTRODUCTION

We are all charged with the responsibility of making choices for ourselves. Sometimes this means making simple choices like deciding which hat to wear, or what flavor ice cream to order; and at other times it means making important choices like deciding not to have sex before marriage or deciding to stop using marijuana. As you can imagine, it is serious choices which deserves our full attention and best reasoning. Serious choices largely determine the depth of our human relationships and the quality of our life in general. Therefore, it is important to know how to properly make a choice and achieve the best outcome.

The Cufflink Formula is designed to teach you the art of making good choices. By learning the nuts-and-bolts of decision-making you become self-empowered and your chances for being successful, while avoiding trouble, increases one-hundredfold! *The Cufflink Formula* uses cufflinks as a symbol for positive choices, and handcuffs as a symbol for negative choices. Each page provides great information that educates you about the various aspects of decision-making and the tools needed for making good choices. The powerful symbols of cufflinks and handcuffs, along with the introduction of newly created terms such as cufflink thoughts, handcuff choices, and cufflink consequences, makes learning the art of decision-making both easy and exciting for all!

The Cufflink Formula model is based on the belief that most of our problems can be effectively solved the exact same way math problems are solved: by using the correct formula. Solving problems using the cufflink formula can help you avoid the perils of rash decision-making, and the dreaded consequences associated with them. The cufflink formula helps produce favorable consequences that you can be proud of at the end of the day.

The material in this book is presented in a manner that makes it interesting and easy to understand. Added to some chapters are short fictional stories called dilemma tales. Each dilemma tale presents a scenario in which a young person faces serious trouble and is challenged with having to make a critical decision. You (along with your friends or group members) are encouraged to become part of each story simply by imagining yourself in the role of one of the main characters and contemplating how to handle the presented dilemma. After reading a story, you should define the main problem and determine the best decision that can be made.

Reading dilemma tales is a safe and effective way to confront serious situations and learn important life-lessons that would otherwise be harmful, and costly, if encountered through a "real-life" experience.
A few of the stories have graphic details. They are included for openly discussing criminal behaviors and consequences that can possibly become a reality for a youth that has lost direction and/or lacks identity and

purpose in life. Deep reflection and open discussion of serious criminal behavior and its consequences is sometimes needed to awaken a young mind that is sidetracked. Each dilemma tale concludes with the powerful question: "What Would You Do?" Additional questions are presented for personal consideration and/or group discussion.

The Cufflink Formula also recognizes and encourages the important use of intuition. Having an inborn knowledge, or gut-feeling, an awareness of something without having to think through every detail, is a form of wisdom acquired from perceptive insight, life experience, and spiritual guidance. The intuitive aspect of decision-making is about trusting the inner voice and following its judgment. The principles of decision-making taught in this book will expand your knowledge and help develop the intuitive senses.

The Cufflink Formula can increase your sense of personal responsibility and accountability by helping you understand the power you have to shape and control your destiny through choices. In today's fast-paced world it is simply not enough just knowing right from wrong. You need to understand how to make a good decision. Investing just a small portion of your time to learn the Cufflink Formula will produce huge returns in the form of knowing how to make awesome choices that lead to the fulfillment of your life's purpose and success. So be encouraged because you will soon learn and master the process!

CHAPTER 1

Cufflinks

What is a cufflink? A cufflink is a stylish fastener that passes through the buttonholes of a shirt to hold its cuff together without overlapping the ends. Cufflinks are made from all types of metals including silver, gold and platinum. They come in different shapes, sizes, colors and styles. The more exposed portion of a cufflink is sometimes monogrammed, decorated with the owner's birthstone, or has an emblem which reflects a vocation or association. Some cufflinks are reasonably priced while custom-made and flashy ones can be expensive.

What kind of person comes to mind when you think of cufflinks? Your answer is not uncommon if you thought of a CEO, lawyer, banker, judge, businesswoman or a professional of some sort. Generally, cufflinks are worn by professional and/or wealthy men and women who like to be stylish and well-dressed. These men and women typically lead productive lives and, therefore, can afford and enjoy quality clothing and stylish accessories like cufflinks and shirt studs. Men and women who wear cufflinks usually have a strong sense of self-confidence and healthy pride. Perhaps it comes from their appreciation for the good choices they made to position themselves to harvest these symbolic fruits of success. In pursuit of their goals these same men and women were confronted with challenging situations that required them to exercise their best judgment. It is because they responded correctly that success came to them in abundance and in due time. Success and its many benefits come only through faith, sacrifice, hard work and good decision-making.

Cufflinks are a symbol of hard work and good decision-making. As a symbol, cufflinks suggest that if you work hard and make good choices you will be rewarded with success. Doing the right things in life and making positive choices is key to creating future happiness and success! This natural law of the universe works for everyone and never changes.

As a young person you will continually experience situations requiring you to make decisions. Each decision you make will affect whatever present situation you are dealing with and can also impact your future by increasing or limiting your opportunities. Therefore, it is important to always make good decisions because consequences often reach far beyond immediate circumstances.

Positive decisions which serve to enhance the quality of yours and other people's lives are considered cufflink decisions. An important key to making a cufflink decision is thinking beforehand about what the consequences of a particular action will be and how those same consequences will impact yourself and others. It is an act of selfless devotion and maturity to consider how your decisions affect the lives of your family members, friends, neighbors and community. It takes character and courage to grow beyond yourself and think about the well-being of other people when making decisions.

A cufflink choice/decision can be easily recognized because of its unique qualities. Its principal quality is that the choice itself steers you away from trouble and promotes positive conduct. For example, if your friend invites you to come along and steal video games and you refuse to do so because you realize it is wrong and will have negative consequences for you, your family and the potential victim, then your decision to say "No" in this situation would be considered a cufflink decision. If you're considering dropping out of school and instead decide to speak with your counselor about getting tutored to help raise your grades, this would also be considered a cufflink decision. And if you are being pressured into becoming sexually active and rather than giving into the pressure you decide to talk about it with your parents or pastor, this too would be a cufflink decision. Cufflink decisions generally produce healthy situational outcomes.

You will always have choices in life and it's your responsibility to make the best decision in every situation. You will be faced with making both minor and major decisions and how you handle these situations will determine your outcome in life. Thinking through situations will empower you to make better decisions. Always remember to think before you act. When you respond to life with cufflink decisions your quality of life and that of others become greatly improved!

Dilemma Tale 1: **Keep Your Eyes on The Prize** (Goals vs Guns)

Seventeen-year-old Thomas was a high school senior, and he played on the football team. Football was his passion. He loved the game. Thomas was the school's star running back and he had recently been offered a couple of scholarships from two colleges on the west coast. Thomas' girlfriend Joya always encouraged him to do well and constantly reminded him that their five-month-old son Tom-Tom was depending on his daddy's success. Thomas lived in a hood where there were two rival gangs that often fought against each other. He didn't like gangs and had taken a pledge to never join one. So far, he had kept his word and was quite proud of it.

One evening Thomas was on his way home from football practice when three gangbangers rode down on him. "What's in the bag, homey?" one of them asked. "Nothing," responded Thomas, trying to sidestep the gangbanger and walk away. Then two other gangbangers closed in with one of them putting a gun in Thomas' face. The thug ordered Thomas to check-in his money, watch and gym shoes. At first Thomas was reluctant. However, he saw his entire life flash before him and quickly did as he was told. He was hoping to avoid getting shot or killed. As Thomas took off his watch the gangbanger hit him in the face and demanded he move faster. A stream of blood and tears began rolling down Thomas' face as he handed over the watch his father had given him. After the thugs took Thomas' things they ran off leaving him bloody and shoeless. Thomas was angry and humiliated.

When Thomas got home his parents immediately took him to the hospital. Afterwards they took him to file a police report. Thomas' mother was extremely emotional about the incident and told him to take another route home to avoid the gangs. Thomas told her, "Mom, it doesn't matter which way I come home, there are gangs all around here." Mom knew he was telling the truth, so she advised him to be as careful as possible. Mom wished they had the money to move away, but she knew they couldn't afford it. Thomas' father also told him to be careful and agreed to pick Thomas up after football practice on the evenings he wasn't working.

A few days later Thomas crossed paths with his friend Quan. Quan had already heard about the robbery and wanted to help Thomas get back at the gangbangers. "What up, fam?", asked Quan, shaking Thomas' hand and embracing him. "I heard a few dudes got down on you last week. What'cha wanna do, fam? We can handle it if you want to," said Quan. Thomas responded, "Bro, I'm just trying to stay focused. My Mom and Dad keep telling me I've got too much to lose." "Well, you won't have anything to lose if those dudes take your life," retorted Quan. Thomas gave thought to what he had just heard; it made sense to him considering how many young people he knew that were victims of gun violence. Suddenly, Quan took out a .40-cal pistol and handed it to Thomas. He told Thomas to always "move with it" just in case someone tried to rob him again. Thomas stared at the gun. Then Quan said, "Man, it's better to get caught with it than without it. Real talk, homey." Quan's logic made sense as Thomas thought about how embarrassed, humiliated and angry he was the night he was robbed. He took the .40-cal burner and left.

The following day after leaving practice Thomas went to visit his son and girlfriend. As he held Thomas Jr. he began thinking about the future. Thomas really wanted to go to college but in the meantime, he just wanted to survive in the hood. As he sat on the couch, he wondered what the future held for him. When Thomas stood, Joya noticed the gun tucked in the small of his back. "What's that, Thomas? I know you are not carrying a gun!!", she yelled. "And I know you haven't brought a gun into my parents' home and around our son!!" Thomas hollered back, "Girl, you want me to die in these streets? You expect me to let those dudes get down on me again? Take my life over nothing?" Joya looked Thomas directly in his eyes and in a very calm voice she said, "Why, baby? We don't need you to ruin your life. We love you." Thomas having no real response blurted out what Quan had said to him the previous day: "Joya, it's better to get caught with it than without it." Joya wasn't feeling his logic. She told him that he needed to think beyond the present and look towards his future. Undecided about what to do, Thomas left and went home.

That night as Thomas laid in bed all kinds of thoughts went through his mind. He knew it was wrong to carry a gun, but he didn't want to get robbed again or possibly killed. Still shaken and angry about the robbery and wanting to feel some sense of security, Thomas considered keeping the gun. Then he thought about his son and Joya's heartfelt words. Thomas also thought about his dream of one day playing football in the NFL. He knew that any run-in with the law would make his dreams go up in smoke. Concerned about saving his opportunity to become a college football star followed by a career at the pro level, Thomas considered returning the gun to Quan. He wondered what he should do.

If you were in Thomas' shoes, what would you do?

Discussion Questions

- Why do you think Thomas pledged to never join a gang? Are you currently in a gang? If so, which one and why did you join?

- How do you think Thomas felt after he was robbed by gangbangers? Have you ever been threatened or assaulted by a gang? If so, how did it make you feel?

- If you were Thomas, would you have accepted the gun from Quan? Why or why not?

- What did Joya mean by telling Thomas to think beyond the present and look towards his future?

- Thomas was carrying a gun around which could potentially ruin his entire future. What is it that you are carrying around [guns, drugs, bad attitude, etc.] that can possibly ruin your future? What changes can you make today that will make your tomorrow better?

Dilemma Tale 2: **Man-Up or Man Down?** (Drugs, Family, and Accountability)

Lil' Kev sat on the sofa watching his brother Darius count all the money he made earlier that day from selling drugs. Darius was nineteen years old and his little brother Kev, who had just turned sixteen, looked up to him. Lil' Kev often tried to talk cool like his brother and he would even wear his brother's baseball caps, jerseys and other fly gear just to be like him. Darius never seemed to mind any of this. He got a kick out of having a "Mini-Me" in his younger sibling.

Darius was making some nice change from selling E-pills and marijuana. His clientele included a few ballers, but he made most of his money from supplying the smaller dealers in his hood. While Darius was making his way in the drug game Lil' Kev was focusing on school and getting good grades. Although he admired his brother's hustle Lil' Kev's dream was to become a doctor. Darius, on the other hand, loved his little brother and always encouraged him to follow his dreams instead of dropping out of school like he had. Their mother was proud of Lil' Kev for doing well in school. Their father, who neither of the boys saw much because he lived out of state, would encourage Lil' Kev whenever he did see him.

One morning Lil' Kev's mother yelled for him to hurry and come on. She was running late for work and had to drop him off at school. Lil' Kev was frantically searching his bedroom for his jacket but couldn't find it. His mother sat in the car constantly honking its horn to make him hurry. When Lil' Kev couldn't find his jacket, he grabbed Darius' new baseball jacket off the end of the bed where he was laying asleep. He figured that his big brother wouldn't mind since Darius had plenty of other jackets in the closet. Besides, he probably wouldn't be getting up until the afternoon anyway. Lil' Kev put the jacket on, ran out the door and hopped in the front seat of his mother's car.

After getting dropped off at school the first-person Lil' Kev ran into was Christie. She was the prettiest girl at Northwestern. They made small talk and walked to the school's entrance where they were required to go through a metal detector and place their book bags onto an X-ray scanner. Christie went through first and waited on the other side for Lil' Kev. He followed, placing his book bag on the scanner and then walking through the metal detector. "Beep, beep, beep, beeeeeeep!!!!", the metal detector sounded. The security guard instructed Lil' Kev to remove anything with metal from his person and go through it again. Lil' Kev removed his belt and walked through. "Beep, beep, beep, beeeeeeep!!!!", it sounded again. As Lil' Kev turned back to try a third time the security guard advised him, "Why don't you remove your jacket, it looks like it has metal buttons. Place it on the X-ray machine." Lil' Kev followed the security guard's orders and placed the jacket onto the scanner. He then walked through the metal detector without a problem and waited on the other side.

The other guard observed the jacket going through the x-ray scanner and noticed something in the inside pocket. "What's that in the pocket?", she asked. Lil' Kev looked confused because he was unaware that something was in the pocket. The guard put her hand inside the jacket and slowly pulled out a clear plastic baggie filled with about four hundred E-pills. She raised her hand high for everyone to see what she had found. At that moment Lil' Kev blurted out, "But those aren't-! And before he could complete his sentence Lil' Kev was thrown up against the wall and arrested. The police came and hauled Lil' Kev away to the local precinct. His mother was informed about the matter and was totally upset because she figured Darius had something to do with it. What role he played she couldn't quite figure out, so she called him. Darius was devastated by the news that his little brother had been busted with his works. He wondered what to do because he was already on two years' probation for drugs and any violation would likely send him straight to prison.

At the police precinct Lil' Kev sat in the holding tank hoping to get out soon and resume his schooling. He knew the drugs weren't his and wondered if his brother would "man up" and take responsibility. But what if Darius chose instead to leave a "man down?", he wondered. Lil' Kev knew of Darius' probation status and didn't want his brother locked away in a prison. However, he also didn't want to ruin his own dream of going to college and becoming a doctor. Lil' Kev and Darius are both faced with a serious dilemma.

If you were in either of their shoes, what would you do?

Discussion Questions

- Who was Lil' Kev's role model? Who is your role model? What is the difference between a positive and negative role model? How should you select a role model for yourself?

- Why was school important to Lil' Kev? What is the connection between school and your positive dreams or goals? Why did Darius encourage his little brother not to drop out of school like he had done? Is there a connection between Darius' choice to drop out of school and him becoming a drug dealer? If so, what is the connection?

- How do drugs affect the quality of life of a person, their family, and the community? Do you have a family member who has a drug problem? If so, how does their situation make you feel? Have you ever used drugs? If so, do you currently use and need help quitting?

- As Lil' Kev was being hauled off to jail for the drugs, what feelings do you think he had towards his big brother? How do you think Darius felt when he learned that his actions affected his little brother? Why is it so important to understand that your actions not only affect you, but also affect others as well?

- What does the term "man up" mean? What does it mean to be responsible and accountable for your actions? What is snitching? Would Lil' Kev be a "snitch" if he told the police that the drugs belonged to Darius? Why or why not? Would it be okay if Darius refused to "man-up" and admit the E-pills belonged to him? Why or why not?

CHAPTER 2

Handcuffs

W hat is a handcuff? Webster's Third International (Unabridged) Dictionary defines a handcuff as a "metal fastening device that is designed to be locked around a wrist, usually connected by a chain, or bar, with another handcuff which can be locked about the other wrist of the same person or the wrist of another person." Handcuffs are usually made from steel or other hard metals and have a graduated locking mechanism that allows for tightening. Once secured onto the wrist, a key is usually required to unlock the handcuff.

Handcuffs are typically used by law enforcement personnel to restrain and control criminals. Handcuffs are a symbol of distrust. Usually those who are placed in them have been accused or found guilty of engaging in unlawful behavior (though there are situations when innocent people are wrongfully placed in handcuffs). Youths that are uneducated, and who live in poverty and commit crimes, have a much greater chance of being placed in handcuffs during adolescence and adult life. Sadly, what this means is that an unfair number of young African-Americans, Latinos, Asians and poor Caucasians in urban areas may likely be placed in handcuffs and eventually end up with criminal records. Pursuing your education and avoiding criminal behavior is a great way to be successful and reduce the chances of being placed in handcuffs.

Many young people feel a false sense of empowerment and excitement when engaging in criminal behavior. Yet, when they get caught for breaking the law and are placed in handcuffs, they naturally feel a great sense of shame and embarrassment. This shame becomes quite evident from the behavior and misguided youth will display once arrested. They'll walk with their head down or will hide their face underneath a shirt or hoodie when reporters with cameras are present. Being handcuffed and hauled off to jail is never a proud moment for anyone. It is embarrassing and deeply humiliating. Consider this: Have you ever witnessed anyone getting arrested and proudly yelling, "Look Mom, I'm on my way to the Big House! I've accomplished my dreams!"? The reason you've never seen such a thing is because getting caught is never part of a wrongdoer's plan. Most people who choose to do wrong don't look that far ahead. If they did, they would realize that the amount of shame and disappointment that comes from going to jail is far more painful and lasts much longer than the temporary thrill received from wrongdoing.

As you experience life you will have to make many decisions for yourself. A decision/choice which produces negative consequences and lessens the quality of life for you and others is known as a "handcuff decision." It is called a handcuff decision because the thought on which it is based is limited in scope and likely doesn't include consideration of how the choice will impact oneself and others. Choices that are based on misinformation or lack of information are also considered handcuff decisions.

Handcuff decision-making instances usually expose you to high-risk situations where the outcome is a tossup between not too good and extremely bad. Negative outcomes (like being expelled from school or going to jail) produced from handcuff decision-making can hurt you today and in the future by reducing or eliminating all together certain opportunities and privileges. Yes! It is true that one handcuff decision alone can be so costly that it can cause you to spend the rest of your life trying to make things right.

While some handcuff decisions are made based on misinformation or lack of information, other handcuff decisions are made out of impulsiveness (by someone choosing to react to a situation without taking enough time to think about how they should respond). To avoid such a decision-making blunder, it would be helpful to learn the *five-second difference* technique. The *five-second difference* (or longer depending on the circumstances) represents a short amount of additional time you provide yourself to correctly judge a tempting or tense situation. It is during this reflection period that you will be able to determine your best choice and decision response. If you are upset or angry the *five-second difference* can provide you with a moment to think about someone or something of more importance than your present situation. This moment of clarity usually helps you gain perspective to make a rational and healthy choice in place of a handcuff decision. *Taking Five* is a good way to prevent yourself from overreacting or reacting without thinking.

Handcuff decisions can result in losing a scholarship, losing a job, expulsion from school, going to jail or even being killed. At all costs avoid making handcuff decisions and protect your future by learning the Cufflink Formula. Remember that any situation requiring you to "make a decision" deserves your full consideration and best choice response.

Dilemma Tale 1: **The Same Thing That Makes You Laugh Makes You Cry** (Crime, Empathy, and Karma)

It was seven o' clock in the morning and nineteen-year-olds Freeze and Loc were trying to make sure the police weren't on to them. They were hard-pressed for money and decided to do an early morning break-in. Freeze turned onto Berkshire Street and was amazed by the beauty of the homes. The manicured lawns, large picture windows and expensive cars in the driveways assured Freeze and Loc there were valuables inside these residences. The homes were plush and expensive just like their homeboy Steel said they would be. Usually Steel would accompany them, but he was at home preparing to report to his probation officer.

Loc spotted an elderly couple backing out of their driveway. After the car turned the corner, Loc and Freeze each put on a mask and approached the home. Loc knocked hard a few times on the side door. When no one answered he jimmied the door open. Freeze gripped the handle of his 9mm pistol, making sure no one would run interference. Once inside they took off in different directions searching for anything of value.

Loc found a gun in the primary bedroom under the mattress. In the next bedroom he noticed someone moving underneath a sheet. The frightened face of a young lady emerged from under the sheet. She was just about to scream when Loc put his finger to his lips and calmly said, "Don't say nothing or I'll have to hurt you." Loc was shocked so he called out for his boy. Freeze came quickly and was shocked too, although for a different reason. Freeze had seen her before but couldn't remember from where. Loc put the gun in his pocket and tied the young lady to the bedpost. He and Freeze then took all the stolen goods and drove to Loc's mother's house.

Freeze left after they divided the stolen goods. Loc chilled in the basement smoking a blunt and was amped up when Steel came by an hour later. The first thing Loc did was tell Steel about the robbery. Steel was upset they went without him because it was against their rules as a crew. He felt left out of the hustle. Loc fired up another blunt and passed it to Steel. Steel took a few hits as Loc went on describing how in the middle of the robbery he was surprised to find a young lady in bed underneath a sheet. Between laughs and chokes from inhaling the blunt, Steel said, "What, man! You ran across Sleeping Beauty while doing a job??!!!" He laughed so hard that his bloodshot eyes were bulging out his head. Loc joined in on the laughter.

About an hour later Steel left and went home. When he got home his cellphone rang. "Hello," he answered. All Steel could hear was crying and the sobbing voice of his girlfriend, Nikki. "What's wrong, baby?", he asked. Nikki stated she was at Providence Hospital and that he needed to get there quickly. "I'm on my way," Steel exclaimed.

Steel arrived at the hospital and was met by Nikki in the lobby of the ER. Nikki explained that her grandparents' home was robbed that morning and that she had been tied up by the robbers. Nikki said her grandmother had a heart attack upon returning home to discover she was tied up and the home robbed. Grandma was now in surgery, and all the family could do was pray and wait. Steel's mind began racing. In his heart he knew this was the same incident he and Loc were laughing about less than an hour earlier. The incident was now staring him in the face, but this time it wasn't funny. Steel was fuming inside because his boys had robbed his girlfriend's family. He felt there was no way Freeze couldn't have recognized Nikki because he had seen her with him on a prior occasion. Steel was wondering about a few things: What would happen to Grandma? Would she live? Should he get revenge on his boys? And what would Nikki think if she knew of his involvement? Nikki tightly hugged Steel and whispered in his ear, "Baby, the police have to find out who did this. Those guys have to pay for this." Steel's eyes became cloudy with tears as he held Nikki close.

If you were in Steel's shoes, what would you do?

Discussion Questions

- Why do you think nineteen-year-olds Freeze and Loc were out at seven a.m. committing a robbery rather than heading to a college campus to attend class?

- How do you think you would feel if someone were to break into your home and steal your valuables? Have you or a family member ever been the victim of a theft crime? How did the experience make you feel? What are some other unfortunate outcomes that can result from breaking into someone's home?

- Why do you think Steel became angry about the robbery only after he found out that it involved his girlfriend and her family?

- Should you be concerned when other people are hurt or violated in some way? Why or why not? What does the word "empathy" mean? Discuss.

- When someone thinks about committing a crime should they consider how they would feel if the same thing were to occur to them? Considering all that happened, does Steel have the right to be angry at his friends Freeze and Loc? Why or why not? What is the worst way this story could end?

Dilemma Tale 2: **Good Girl Gone Bad** (Dreams, Drugs, Love, and Loyalty)

Zena was seventeen years old and had the potential to be anything she wanted. Her dream was to study journalism at Spellman University in Atlanta. For the past year Zena had been dating Navarro. He was nineteen years old. Navarro became Zena's first love and meant the world to her. In her heart she felt they would be together forever. Navarro was feeling Zena and liked that she was trustworthy and dependable.

Zena and Navarro spent lots of time together. Zena and Navarro were together even more when her mother was unfortunately killed at the hands of a drunk driver. Navarro was by Zena's side providing comfort and helping her see things in a positive light as much as he could. When Zena's family fell short on cash to pay for her mother's headstone Navarro stepped up and paid for it. Zena appreciated this and admired him. The reason Navarro was able to do so much for Zena was because he made plenty of money supplying prescription pills to the smaller drug dealers in the hood. Zena was aware of what he did to make money, but she never questioned him about his street business. Turning a blind eye to her boyfriend's illegal pharmacy meant that it didn't exist; and if it didn't exist, she owed no responsibility to herself or anyone to justify why she had chosen to be involved with a drug dealer. They were bonded and nothing and no one seemed to come between them.

Sometimes Zena would speak to Navarro about her dream of attending Spellman. In response, Navarro would express that he wanted her to attend a local college so they could maintain their closeness. Zena's feelings for Navarro ran deep and were based on love and loyalty, the kind where one person is willing to take a bullet for the one they love. She began questioning going to Spellman and considered going to a local college. Zena wrestled with the inner conflict of her dreams and affairs of the heart while Navarro stayed focused on expanding his street business. Then it happened as only fate could dictate. Zena had to decide whether to become involved or remain uninvolved with her boyfriend's criminal dealings. Navarro was becoming too busy to make all his drop-offs and pick-ups in the 'hood, so he asked Zena to make these short runs for him. Out of loyalty, love and a deep sense of obligation she agreed to occasionally do short runs for him. After a month or so Zena became caught up in the routine of regularly handling packages. Navarro compensated her with jewelry and extra cash that she wasn't used to having but was beginning to enjoy. Much to her own surprise she found herself not only enjoying the money but truly liking the thrill of hustling and being Navarro's ride-or-die chick.

Zena began thinking about how life would be without Navarro if she relocated to Atlanta to attend Spellman. Eventually she completely bought into Navarro's vision for her to attend college locally to pursue her dream of becoming a journalist. After high school graduation Zena officially canceled her plans for Spellman and enrolled at Wayne State University (WSU). She figured her new plan would allow her to have the best of both worlds – attend college and still be with her boyfriend. When fall semester got underway Zena found it a little difficult to juggle classes and maintain an exciting love and hustle relationship with Navarro. Though it was a challenge she did fairly-well in the fall semester.

Winter semester went by just as quickly as it had come. On the last day of the semester Zena had final exams. She was running behind for class because she had agreed to make a last-minute "drop-off" for Navarro. Because the dealer didn't show up, Zena was forced to hold onto the drugs. She couldn't go back to Navarro's house because she didn't want to run the risk of being late and missing finals. Zena drove onto campus a few minutes behind schedule, carelessly flung the clear baggie of pills underneath the driver's seat and then headed to class at a fast pace.

Once Zena had finished taking her finals she walked to the parking lot. She discovered the police were inspecting her car. After the campus police identified her, she was placed under arrest for possession of a controlled substance. Zena later learned that she had failed to put the baggie completely underneath the seat and had left it in plain view on the floor mat. After being taken to the precinct she was interrogated by two female detectives. They discovered Zena had no criminal record and therefore didn't believe the drugs belonged to her. The detectives wanted to know why she had them and who they belonged to? To get Zena to come clean the detectives threatened her with lifetime expulsion from WSU and five years jail time. They told her if she cooperated, she would receive academic probation for one year and no criminal charges would be brought against her. Zena couldn't believe what was happening, so she closed her eyes, rocked back in her chair, and then said a silent prayer.

If you were in Zena's shoes, what would you do?

Discussion Questions

- Why is it important to have a life dream? What life dream do you have and what must you do to make it your reality?

- What are the risks Zena faces when being involved with a drug dealer?

- Did Navarro's actions reflect that he really loved Zena? How so?

- What harm do drugs cause to individuals, families, and communities?

- How can you best protect your life dreams and future? What is loyalty? What does it mean to be loyal to yourself first?

CHAPTER 3

Choices

"Who we are in the present is the result of the choices we made in the past. Who we'll become in the future is the result of the choices we'll make today." ~ Author unknown

LIFE WITHOUT CHOICES

How exciting would life be if we didn't have choices? Imagine for a second, going to your favorite restaurant and learning they have a new menu that consists only of one entree and nothing more. It probably would be fair to say that your dining experience would be boring, and you might choose to never eat there again. Now imagine if everyone was required to wear the exact same outfit every day. This would result in having no opportunity to express your personal swagger as it relates to clothes and fashion. And how cool do you think it would be if everyone had to listen to one kind of music? Lovers of hip-hop would likely become extremely bored if required to listen only to classical music; and a constant diet of hip-hop would likely be a humdrum experience for lovers of country music. Finally, consider how unhappy life would be if a total stranger had absolute authority to make every choice for you. Just from these few examples you can imagine that life without choices would be dull, uninteresting, and dissatisfying.

THE BENEFIT OF CHOICES

Choices are a real blessing because every person can select what best suits their individual tastes, preferences, and interests. The benefit of having choices is that you don't have to be subjected to what other people want for you. *You* alone have the privilege and power to control much of what you will experience in life. Having choices means you have a degree of personal authority over your path and can shape your life the way you like.

SACRED TRUST

Choice-making is a personal and sacred trust given as a birthright and developed over time. The basis of this sacred trust is that at mid-adolescence you must begin assuming responsibility for making positive and important choices for yourself that lead to the construction of a good future. Preparation for responsibly handling this sacred trust is to be provided by the collective of parents, teachers, and other positive authority figures in your life.

Honoring your sacred trust usually begins at a time when your search for individual identity and purpose is underway. Searching for identity and purpose can make the responsibility of positive choice-making challenging. Young people who place an abundance of stock into what their friends think about them are more likely to make important choices from a peer-influenced standpoint as opposed to a value-based or purpose-driven one.

Unfortunately, this happens to so many young people who choose to follow the crowd. They seek to fit in rather than *choosing* to stand on their own and pursue their dreams. Honoring your sacred trust of positive choice-making requires that you love yourself more than you fear getting teased by others or rejected by them.

Helpful to upholding your sacred trust of choice-making is understanding the direct connection between choices and life circumstances. Each important choice you make in life either enhances or diminishes your human potential and produces consequences that reflect the quality of each given choice. Positive (cufflink) choices usually produce healthy situational outcomes, and negative (handcuff) choices usually result in unhealthy situational outcomes. Therefore, the brightness or darkness of your future is determined by how well you observe your sacred trust of choice/decision-making. Take your responsibility seriously and think of your positive choices as building blocks for the making of a great future you'll be proud of and happy to live!

TYPES OF CHOICES

Reflexive Choices

Reflexive choices are basically routine-based responses used to address pressing life issues and problems. For example, a driver approaching a traffic signal changing from yellow to red would likely respond *reflexively* by removing his/her foot from the gas pedal and applying the brake. This makes the vehicle come to a complete stop, helping the driver avoid an accident with cars in the intersection. This common response (choice) although reflexive in appearance is actually rooted in prior knowledge from direct experience or observation. As such, it has already been sufficiently thought-out well before its use in any present tense situation. Reflexive choices are often referred to as *no-brainers*. This is because they can be quickly made without the need for intense reasoning or long deliberation. In fact, overthinking in a situation that calls for reflexive choice-making could prove dangerous. These types of choices give flow to life and allow people to respond to unplanned emergencies in a timely manner.

Preference Choices

Daily each of us makes preference choices based on our personal likes and dislikes. This occurs from the moment we get up in the morning until the time we retire at night. Our daily preference choices may start with determining what clothes to wear and end with deciding what book to read or television show to watch before we go to sleep. These personal choices are known as *preference choices* because they reflect what we individually prefer.

Generally, most preference choices are non-serious and self-affective. This means they are usually harmless and impact only the person making the choice. However, when our preference choices are illogical, irrational, and selfish, they can negatively impact others. For example, a father who chooses to smoke weed and then loses his good-paying job because he fails a drug test will create bad consequences for himself and his family who financially depend on him. Likewise, a teenage star athlete who violates a school rule and gets suspended the day before the school's team game will hurt not only himself but his teammates. A suspension prevents him from contributing to the team's collective effort to win. We all have the right to make our own preference choices, but before we make them, we should consider how they may affect others. Though preference choices are personal we should never make them for selfish reasons.

Cooperative Choices

Cooperative choices are made by two or more people who *cooperate* with each other in deciding how to address an important life issue or problem. Some common examples of cooperative choice-making are: (1) coworkers handling a joint project; (2) parents deciding how to discipline their child; or (3) a team of basketball players deciding the best play to run on their last possession of a game.

Cooperative choice-making requires the use of optional and critical thinking (to be discussed in Chapter 7, The Cufflink Formula). There may be a time frame involved in the cooperative process, but still each rendered decision should be made with careful thought and deliberation. The outcomes of cooperative choices typically affect the parties involved in making them (and in some instances other people, too); however, the end goal of cooperative choice-making is to carry out the best decision that serves the collective values and interests of all parties involved.

Authoritative Choices

Authoritative choices are major decisions which have consequences that affect the quality and direction of your life's course. In other words, these are serious choices with outcomes powerful enough to influence how you view and feel about life itself. This in turn can ultimately influence the path you decide to take in life. It is for these reasons that authoritative choices have a higher risk-reward factor than other choices. The more serious an authoritative choice the greater the payoff or punishment according to how you decide.

Making well thought-out and positive authoritative choices will likely result in you harvesting great rewards of personal happiness and pleasant life circumstances. On the other hand, making negative and not well-thought-out authoritative choices will likely result in you reaping personal misfortunes and miserable life circumstances.

Authoritative choices affect our lives in significant ways and therefore should always be addressed using The Cufflink Formula decision-making model. Using this highly effective model will ensure your consideration of both short and long-term consequences and increase your probability of making an informed and good decision.

Most adolescents eventually inherit the personal responsibility of having to make authoritative choices. Sometimes this personal responsibility is earned and in other instances it is birthed out of the necessity to survive. Regardless of how you or someone else has come into the responsibility of having to make authoritative choices, the key for any smart decision-maker is recognizing this responsibility exists and respecting it by using a proven and positive problem-solving formula. Approaching decision-making from this standpoint will help you understand and appreciate the cardinal rule that every individual must be responsible and accountable for the choices he/she makes (or fails to make). This cardinal rule is based on the principle that no individual should endure favorably or unfavorably any consequence created by the hands of another. For whomsoever puts forth great effort in making a good authoritative choice deserves to be rewarded; accordingly, and whomsoever fails to put forth a great effort and makes a reckless authoritative choice deserves to be compensated accordingly. Clearly a choice can have rewarding or punishing consequences. Therefore, it helps any right-minded person to respect the process of decision-making by taking it seriously. Be mindful and smart when making an authoritative choice because its consequences can sometimes last a lifetime.

The root word of *authoritative* is "author." The word *author* comes from the Latin word *auctor*, which means "creator". Thus, it is through our own authoritative choices that each of us essentially becomes the *creator* of our own life circumstances, be it for better or worse. The phrase *authoritative choice* is a Cufflink Formula term. It aligns with the age-old belief that everyone has the right and the personal "authority to choose" the life they want for themselves. Authoritative choices represent the power you have within to build the life you "choose." You are the great architect of your own future so use your authoritative choices to build the life you truly deserve!

Authoritative choices require your serious attention, patience, and sober thinking skills. Due to the impactful consequences of these choices a person should never make them in haste, while angry or even when over-excited. These emotional phases are fleeting and can disrupt the decision-making process by clouding your judgment. Think clearly through each authoritative choice-making situation and consider how the consequences of an opposite choice could order your life steps. To see how this works, review and consider how the consequences of each of the following examples of opposite life choices would affect your life differently: Making the choice to (1) graduate or drop out of school; (2) practice sexual abstinence or become sexually active; (3) work an honest job or steal; (4) go to college or hang in the streets; (5) obey the law or commit a crime; (6) become a mentor to a younger person or have/make a baby; or (7) join the ranks of the school honor roll or join a street gang. These seven examples are just a snapshot of the many challenging and opposing choices that young people face every day. Although it should be clear that negative consequences will result from each of the latter choices, the fact is that many youths will still gravitate to those choices because of low self-esteem or lack of knowledge. For some young people it is a difficult challenge to make positive authoritative decisions. Perhaps a huge part of the reason for this is because they haven't been taught the wonderful art of cufflink decision-making. This critical deficit in the average adolescent's educational experience is why there is a great need and demand for the powerful decision-making lessons presented in this book. By continuing to read this book you will learn how to properly make authoritative choices. Good decisions will help lead you to a quality life filled with purpose and happiness.

GOVERNING SELF

Having the authority to control your range of experiences is an awesome power and privilege. It means you can self-govern rather than have an outside entity govern you. Governing yourself simply means regulating and controlling your own affairs. This includes keeping up high standards of health, education, social interaction, and spiritual awareness. Your parents or guardians governed your affairs one hundred percent of the time when you are young. It is their responsibility to decide what you eat, what school you attend, which church you join and in some instances who will be your friends. However, your parents' or guardians' goal is to teach you to make good decisions and then pass that responsibility onto you. Basically, your parents or guardian provide you with the opportunity to earn the right to govern and control the affairs of your own life.

CUFFLINK JUDGMENT

Taking on the important responsibility of governing yourself calls for use of cufflink judgment. So, what is cufflink judgment? Cufflink judgment is simply using your mind to come to an honest, balanced and factually based conclusion as to the best course of action to address any given problem or situation. It is one of the handy problem-solving tools in your toolbox. If you use it regularly it remains in good working condition instead of becoming rusty and transforming into handcuff judgment. Having cufflink judgment can help you intelligently measure a set of choices, distinguishing those options which likely lead to cufflink consequences from those that lead to handcuff consequences.

Using cufflink judgment helps you identify positive choices that lead to the accomplishment of your goals; and it also helps identify and weed out negative choices that can choke your dreams and destroy your life. The main key to exercising cufflink judgment rests upon your ability to: 1) think positive and consider your complete range of options [choices]; 2) evaluate the likely outcomes of those options, narrowing them down to the best two; and lastly, 3) decide and carry out the single best option which most constructively enhances the quality of your life and the people around you. Cufflink judgment comes from using optional, critical, and consequential thinking techniques (to be discussed in Chapter 7, The Cufflink Formula). Becoming familiar with these processes will help you become a sharp and wise cufflink decision-maker!

INTUITIVE JUDGMENT

There are many ways of knowing things and intuition is one of them. Intuition is the ability to know without having to resort to reasoning. It is the unexplainable gut feeling of certainty we often experience when making a serious determination about something or someone. Intuition is a form of spiritual guidance that helps direct our decision-making whenever we reach the crossroads of fate and destiny in life. Intuition is born out of the sweet mixture of each person's present awareness, life experiences, and spiritual enlightenment. It is independent of logical reasoning because the divine or supernatural is often beyond our ordinary understanding and, as such, is difficult to explain. Intuitive judgments are those moments in which we experience a deep inner conviction about something without necessarily understanding why and without having all the facts. We just know what we know. Intuition is a higher form of "knowing" that requires trusting your inner feelings and following your "first mind." Do not be afraid to yield to the intuitive voice when it speaks boldly to you because it is usually suggesting the right choice.

HANDCUFF JUDGMENT

Handcuff judgment is the direct opposite of cufflink judgment. It is the inevitable result of what occurs when the two deadly poisons of irresponsibility and faulty thinking become the basis for decision-making. Irresponsibility shows up in decision-making in the manner of having a blatant disregard for the consequences of your choices. Making serious choices based solely on how you *feel* or on what you *assume* rather than on facts is irresponsible, dangerous and must be avoided! Faulty thinking (refusing to seek the truth and instead depending on misinformation or lack of information to make a choice) is unwise, risky, and leads to troublesome outcomes. It is practically impossible to reach an honest and balanced perspective regarding the options of a choice-making situation when facts have been substituted with untruths. Narrow thinking patterns interfere with good reasoning and limit your creative ability to seek solutions to solvable problems. Handcuff judgment tends to make negative choices alluring and makes positive ones seem unattractive or unattainable. Make it your business to resist relying on handcuff judgment when making decisions.

MOTIVES

What makes anyone select one choice and reject another? The answer is as simple as 1, 2, 3, motive! That's right. For every serious choice you make there is always a "motive" or a reason for why you make it. The motive may be an emotional, mental, physical, or spiritual need that incites or inspires you to make a specific choice.

Identifying and examining your motive(s) before making an important decision can provide you with valuable insight. It can help you understand the basis of your intentions as well as the reasonableness of any choice you're considering. Examining your motive(s) is a helpful precaution which provides an added opportunity for reflection before committing to a particular course of action. Having the advantage of a second reflection to pre-determine how you will respond to a challenging life situation can make a huge difference in the outcome. Understanding your motives can help prevent you from making the wrong choice and can strengthen your conviction for making the right one. People who don't have a clue of their motives are more likely to make the wrong choice or make a choice for the wrong reason. Failing to consider up front the "why" (motive) behind a particular choice greatly decreases your ability to weigh the correctness or incorrectness of the choice. Avoid the practice of considering what your motive is only after you've made a poor choice and endured hurtful consequences. This is referred to as "backwards thinking."

When making an important choice take time to consider your primary motive. Is it your commitment to a positive goal or dream you have? Your commitment to religious beliefs? Could it be to demonstrate loyalty to your homeboys or homegirls? Is it the good feeling of acceptance and cool points you receive from friends? Is it personal pride? Motives are the driving factors of decision-making. As such, they influence which choices you'll consider and which ones you'll ultimately make. If your motives are positive and values/spiritual-based then it is very likely your choice, and its consequences will also be positive. However, if your motives are negative, selfish, and based on the code of the streets then you can expect your choice and its consequences to be negative. Simply put, having a good motive will likely lead you to a correct choice; and having a bad motive will likely lead to an incorrect choice. Asking and answering the motive question beforehand increases your level of self-awareness and empowers you to be consciously in charge when making important choices. Cufflink decision-makers are always aware of what their motives are "prior" to making important choices and decisions.

THE UNGOVERNED SELF

Anyone that fails to take on the responsibility of governing themselves will continue having other people rule over them. They will likely find themselves in the position of having judicial and law enforcement authorities control every aspect of their lives. Being under the authority of the courts and jail system is very degrading, humiliating and torturing to one's spirit. The experience is worse than a repeated nightmare. Do not make choices that risk your freedom and can land you behind bars where strangers are responsible for making choices for you.

The ungoverned self is the product of being undisciplined in thought and deed. When your thought process is distorted and unfocused it will likely gravitate to anything negative and to trouble. To prevent falling into this trap you must divorce handcuff thinking, refrain from taking handcuff chances and refuse to make a handcuff decision for any reason! Regulate and control yourself or someone else will regulate and control you!

GROWTH FROM YOUR CHOICES

Every choice you've made can help you learn more about yourself. Reviewing past choices and examining the reasons why you made them is like looking in a mirror to see a clear image of yourself. This kind of self-reflection can provide valuable insight as it relates to your character and thinking. It can even help you recognize your inner strengths and weaknesses regarding decision-making. Looking within yourself and viewing each decision as an outward expression of a positive or negative belief will help you understand that making positive changes in your life through choices start first on the inside. This awareness should inspire you to adopt positive affirmations to reinforce positive beliefs (strengths) and should motivate you to rid yourself of negative thoughts that support negative beliefs (weaknesses). Making this adjustment in your thinking improves your behavior, character and decision-making!

Exercise: **Payoff Chances** (Dollars & Cents)

Dear Gifted Young Person:

Good morning! Our company Rocklyn Diamond Jewelry, Inc. makes stylish custom-made jewelry for men and women across the United States and around the world. We make our unique jewelry in our factory right here in your hometown. Currently business is booming, and we are short on workers. Therefore, to meet high customer demand we must hire a few new employees that can work temporarily for just 31 days. This job might be perfect for you if you would like to earn a decent amount of cash for yourself in a short time.

Because the job is temporary and lasts only 31 days, we are showing our appreciation to each new employee joining our team by allowing them to choose one of two payment plan options. Please read both payment plans. If you're interested in working, simply choose the plan you prefer by writing your initials next to it.

_____PLAN A: Immediate payment of $100,000.00 for signed agreement to work a complete month consisting of 31 days. On the 1st day of work, you SHALL receive in your bank account a cash deposit in the total amount of One Hundred-Thousand Dollars ($100,000.00). This money can be accessed by you only after you have completed 31 days of work.

or

_____ PLAN B: Delayed payment of double-penny investment for signed agreement to work a complete month consisting of 31 days. This plan pays you one penny on your first day, doubles the penny to two cents on your second day, doubles two cents to four cents on your third day, doubles four cents to eight cents on your fourth day, doubles eight cents to sixteen cents on your fifth day of work and continues to double your pay everyday thereafter for 31 days. At the conclusion of the 31st working day you SHALL receive cash totaling the amount of your double-penny investment for 31 days of work.

_____ After having read both payment options if you decide you don't like Plan A or Plan B and do not want to work, simply initial here.

✫   ✫   ✫

If you selected a plan, explain why you think the one you chose was best. Plan A's offer of $100,000.00 equals a daily wage of about $3,225.80. This is great money for making stylish custom-made jewelry! Due to the large sum of money offered ($100,000.00), it probably didn't take you long to recognize this as a great financial opportunity.

Plan B's double-penny investment option starting at one cent probably sounded absurd and unworthy of any real consideration. On the surface this option isn't as appealing as Plan A. However, if you look at the following 31-day progressive payment chart you will see how the double-penny investment option of Plan B is a much better choice than the $100,000.00 payment option offered under Plan A. The progressive payment chart reflects that under Plan B an employee can earn more than ten million dollars in just one month! Let's check it out:

PROGRESSIVE PAYMENT CHART

Day 1	0.01	Day 16	$ 327.68
Day 2	0.02	Day 17	$ 655.36
Day 3	0.04	Day 18	$ 1,310.72
Day 4	0.08	Day 19	$ 2,621.44
Day 5	0.16	Day 20	$ 5,242.88
Day 6	0.32	Day 21	$ 10,485.76
Day 7	0.64	Day 22	$ 20,971.52
Day 8	$ 1.28	Day 23	$ 41,943.04
Day 9	$ 2.56	Day 24	$ 83,886.08
Day 10	$ 5.12	Day 25	$ 167,772.16
Day 11	$ 10.24	Day 26	$ 335,544.32
Day 12	$ 20.48	Day 27	$ 671,088.64
Day 13	$ 40.96	Day 28	$ 1,342,177.28
Day 14	$ 81.92	Day 29	$ 2,684,354.56
Day 15	$ 163.84	Day 30	$ 5,368,709.12
		Day 31	$10,737,418.24

Imagine that! Many people automatically choose Plan A over Plan B because it sounds like a great deal and offers a decent amount of money. As this exercise clearly demonstrates, it really does pay off to resist going along with a choice simply because it sounds good! You need to always think deeply (critically) about important choices for two reasons: (1) so you can fully benefit from the positive opportunities presented to you; and (2) so you can avoid the traps that come from shallow thinking and impulsive decision-making.

Gifted young person, the point of this exercise is to help you realize the benefit of thinking more in depth when making important choices. There's an old saying that goes, "Everything that glitters isn't gold." This means that just because something [or someone] looks or sounds good doesn't necessarily make it [or them] the right choice for you. Another saying goes, "You must remove the lid from the pot to actually *know* what's cooking inside." In other words, the key to making good decisions begins with becoming disciplined in your thinking so that your focus is on gaining understanding and appreciation for all the facts and likely consequences of each choice. This calls for resisting the temptation of making choices solely because their results make you feel good or provide some other form of instant reward. Good decision-making is all about looking deeper into choices prior to making a decision. When we make our final decision, we want to make it with confidence. Continue reading if you want to learn the Cufflink Formula model and be successful in life!

CHAPTER 4

Root Values

Everyone has a personal belief system. Your personal belief system consists of the total collection of thoughts and ideas you have about what you *believe* is right or wrong, fair, or unfair, and important or unimportant in life. These personal beliefs referred to as root values become the basis for the way you think and how you conduct yourself. Root values, therefore, are a set of principles -- whether positive or negative -- that you aspire to live up to.

Your first set of root values usually comes from your parents and other family members. Your parents teach you principles and model behaviors for you during your early years. The principles you learn and adopt from home are basically a carbon copy of the ideas and understanding your parents have about life. Thus, your parents become the living blueprint from which you learn to conduct yourself and by which you interpret other people's behaviors. However, as you get a little older your associations, schooling, culture and the environment in which you live begin to play a deeper role in shaping your root values. The ideas and behaviors you see commonly practiced by those in your surroundings reflect the collective root values and possibilities of the larger community. These collective root values can be positive or negative in quality and may, or may not, mirror the principles you were taught at home. Therefore, it is up to you to decide which root values you will adopt or reject.

How you respond to the ongoing drama of life is based on your root values. Root values are the lenses through which you view life and interpret its events. How you see a situation is directly connected to the way you choose to respond to it. For example, if two young guys are standing at a bus stop and a third fellow approaches and calls them "punks," the responses they give can be quite different based on their individual root values. Considering one young guy is a good student and has "self-confidence" as one of his root values, and the other young guy is a street thug who has "distrust" and "hate" as one of his root values, how might their individual responses to the same situation differ? The young student being very confident of himself would likely consider the insult meaningless and ignore it altogether. Yet, the young street thug would probably take the insult personally and respond angrily because he views it as a direct challenge to his image. Same scenario, but two different responses. Simply stated, your behavior is the outward expression of your personal beliefs (root values).

The roots of oak trees are long and extend deep into the earth. These long roots help keep the tree grounded and secure. Similarly, your collective root values (positive or negative) extend deep into the regions of your mind and spirit and keep you grounded in relative patterns of thinking and behavior. Positive root values reinforce patterns of healthy thinking and promote cufflink decision-making. And negative root values reinforce patterns of unhealthy thinking and lead to handcuff decision-making. Adopting positive root values can help you build a healthy relationship with yourself, others, and the world around you. On the other hand, adopting negative root values damages your relationship with self, others, and the world around you.

Take a moment and complete the "10-Point Root Values Mirror" to gain insight into your own thinking and behavior. The mirror exercise is a values clarification exercise that can provide you with a clear picture of who you are by helping you identify your top ten root values. When you honestly acknowledge what your root values are you can then determine whether you need to make changes. For we can only change those beliefs and behaviors that we are willing to acknowledge! So, take a few minutes and fill in the 10-Point Root Values Mirror by writing down in your own words your top ten root values. To help you get started with your list of root values, here are a few examples: Honesty, loyalty, kindness, self-love, respect, no-snitching, spirituality, thug life, hustling, money, no crying, fairness, family, education, stealing, and happiness. Keep in mind, it is okay to use words that describe the type of person you're aiming to be.

⋆   ⋆   ⋆

10-POINT ROOT VALUES MIRROR

1. _____

2. _____   6. _____

3. _____   7. _____

4. _____   8. _____

5. _____   9. _____

10. _____

Now that you have filled in the 10-Point Root Values Mirror, how do you honestly feel about what your character portrait reflects? Does the portrait make you feel happy? Disappointed? Angry? Satisfied? Confused? Hopefully your character portrait makes you feel good about yourself. But if it doesn't, the good news is you have the opportunity and the power to change it right now! Having made an honest evaluation of your character you can now find out if your root values are working for or against you. In other words, you can determine which root values help you achieve your dreams, and which ones push you further away from your dreams. Consider the root values on your list that promote good behavior. These are the root values you should maintain. But those root values you've written down that promote trouble in your life need to be abandoned and replaced with positive ones. Why? Because positive root values will springboard you on the path of success and help you accomplish your dreams and goals in life.

If you want to live right but continually find yourself making handcuff decisions, it is likely your aspirations for success and root values are in conflict. A person who wants to be a lawyer but believes in breaking the law is conflicted. When your aspirations and root values don't align, it is usually your root values that have the stronger influence. The old saying, "As a man thinketh, so is he" rings true, and it confirms that our root values are what determines our thinking and behavior. Your root values must be positive if you wish to accomplish positive goals in life, so replace any negative root values you have with positive ones. This will increase your self-esteem, improve the quality of your choices, and also help you present your best self to the world.

Group Values

Positive root values are meant to help you stay grounded in good behavior. So why is it that when we're around our peers it becomes easier to abandon our positive root values and make boneheaded decisions that we can later find ourselves ashamed of? The answer is quite simple: group values. When a certain member (or members) of a peer group has dominant influence and negative root values, other members with less influence in the group may feel pressured or intimidated to follow along should the leaders decide to engage in criminal behavior. The very conduct you normally would not do as an individual can become the very thing you end up doing when you are part of a group or in the company of someone who has a strong influence upon you. For example, if you don't believe in stealing and your friends encourage or dare you to shoplift from a store, their hype and pressure for you to steal may be just enough to convince you at that moment to do the very thing you would never think of doing if alone.

Approval feels so important in the moment. Trying to fit in and be accepted among your peers is not a good reason for making a bad decision. Sometimes peer groups can intimidate, create false courage, and foster disregard for what is morally and spiritually right. Therefore, be mindful to think for yourself and always stick to your positive root values, especially when feeling pressured from peer group members. Remember the following advice when faced with making a decision that does not feel right to you: "Whether I am alone or with others, I am responsible for doing the right thing."

Dilemma Tale 1: **It's So Hard to Say Goodbye** (Domestic Violence)

DeMontre was sixteen years old. For as long as he could remember he witnessed his mother being abused at the hands of his father. Although DeMontre (who everyone called Trey) loved his father, there was a part of his dad --the violent side-- that he hated. It was the cruel side of his father that caused Trey to promise himself never to abuse women.

Trey was getting good grades during his junior year of high school. Around this time, he met an attractive girl named Trisha in the school cafeteria. Trisha was also sixteen and was being raised by her mother; her father had never been in her life. Trey and Trisha hit it off well and in a short time they became a couple.

Trey and Trisha looked like the perfect pair of high school kids in love. Then one day all of that changed when Trey walked into the cafeteria and saw Trisha talking and laughing with a new boy who had recently transferred to the school. Trey approached them and shouted, " What the hell is going on, Trisha? Shocked by his strange behavior, Trisha sternly responded, "What does it look like, Trey? I'm having a conversation!" Trey grabbed Trisha's arm and pulled her up from the seat. As they exchanged heated words, Trey marched Trisha out into the hallway. At first Trisha resisted, but her struggle quickly gave way to the wave of embarrassment she felt from onlookers. She didn't want to make a scene. Outside the cafeteria Trey repeatedly yelled at Trisha, accusing her of having an interest in the boy she'd been talking with when Trey arrived. Eventually Trey calmed down and apologized. Trisha forgave him.

Trey and Trisha continued dating as the school year went on. However, there continued to be episodes in which Trey felt insecure and accused Trisha of lying and cheating. Trey became more abusive by calling Trisha names and throwing things at her. Trisha became scared of her boyfriend, but she wouldn't leave him because she was in love and felt she needed him. Trey was the first guy who ever made Trisha feel beautiful and he was also her first and only sexual partner.

Trey began to realize that he was acting more like his father. He knew that he had broken a major promise to himself. However, thinking about it did nothing but make him feel worthless and out of control. That's why after each time that he was verbally and physically abusive, he would cry, apologize, and beg for Trisha's forgiveness. In the beginning his tears and remorse seemed genuine. Yet, with time Trisha learned Trey's apologies were just empty words he would use to get back into her good grace. The advice Trisha once received from an old lady repeated in her head: "Love is never supposed to hurt, dear. Love is never supposed to hurt ..." It was near the end of the school year when Trey ended up hitting Trisha in her face.

At that point Trisha decided she had enough and told Trey their relationship was over for good. Trisha avoided him and ignored his text messages and calls.

Two weeks later Trisha was with some friends at the local skating rink. That same evening Trey and his boys happened to show up there. Trey instantly became filled with jealousy and rage when he saw Trisha skating with her male friend. He felt disrespected by Trisha and thought he looked like a fool to his friends. He believed that he and Trisha would soon get back together again like they had done so many times before. Trey felt even worse when one of his boys asked him, "Isn't that your girl skating with that dude, Trey?"

As Trisha and her male friend walked to the refreshment counter, Trey walked up and stood directly in her path. He grabbed Trisha so hard that he broke her shoulder strap on her shirt. Justly angered, Trisha yelled, "Now look what you've done, Trey! You need to stop trippin', I'm no longer with you!" Ignoring her words, Trey shouted back, "You're leaving right now with me!" When Trisha's male friend tried to intervene Trey sternly warned him to mind his own business. As Trey forcefully pulled Trisha away, he seethed into her ear the following words: " You're always going to be mine." Knowing that lately Trey was becoming more violent, Trisha felt extremely afraid of what Trey would do if she refused his orders. Trisha was also scared of what she might face if she walked outside with him. She trembled, realizing she only had seconds to make a decision.

If you were in Trisha's shoes, what would you do?

Discussion Questions

- What is domestic violence? Have you ever witnessed or been involved in a domestic violence situation? Explain please.

- How do you think Trisha feels? What should she do to get help in this situation?

- Why do you think Trey broke the promise he made to himself? Where did Trey learn how to treat women? Who taught you how a woman is to be treated? How does television, music, and other forms of entertainment influence the way we think about women?

- How would you feel if what happened to Trisha were to happen to your mother or sister?

- How can you get help for yourself, or someone else that is in a domestic violence situation?

- If you or someone you know is experiencing domestic abuse, contact the National Domestic Violence Hotline at 1-800-799-7233. The hotline is available 24 hours a day, 7 days a week. You are not alone.

Dilemma Tale 2: **He Loves Me, He Loves Me Not?** (Personal Values, Sex, & Acceptance)

Fifteen-year-old Amber was a sophomore at Mumford High School. She lived with her parents who both worked and regularly attended church. Amber was a member of the church's youth choir. Her amazing voice drew plenty of praise from everyone that heard her sing.

One day at school, Amber and her girlfriends gathered by their lockers and sang a popular song. Seventeen-year-old Drew, the captain of the school's basketball team, walked up and heard them harmonizing. Drew became instantly attracted to Amber. He started a conversation with her and by the end of their talk they had exchanged numbers.

For the next couple of months, Amber and Drew talked daily. Amber was excited to have drawn the attention of the most popular senior in school. When her parents learned of her interest in Drew, they decided they needed to meet him. Amber's parents always reminded her of the Pure Flower Pledge she took to remain a virgin until she married. Amber always acknowledged her parents' reminder and assured them she would keep her spiritual commitment of abstinence.

Amber and Drew continued dating throughout the school year, confessing their love and spending lots of time together. They often cuddled and kissed, but out of respect for Amber's abstinence commitment the pair never took it any further. Graduation was nearing so Drew began wondering if he should take someone other than Amber to the prom. He wanted to have sex on prom night like the rest of his male friends were planning. The problem was that he knew Amber likely wouldn't be willing.

When Drew mentioned to Amber that he wanted to have sex on prom night, she reminded him of the pledge she had taken. Drew rejected her reasoning and tried to convince Amber that she should give up her virginity, "if she really loved him." He expressed how much he loved her and argued that the pledge shouldn't stand in the way of them having sex since they planned to marry each other in the future anyway. When this approach didn't work, Drew told Amber to stop acting like a little girl and grow up by having sex with the man she loves. He also told Amber she was depriving him of sex and promised to leave her if she wasn't willing to "give it up."

Amber deeply cared for Drew and didn't want to lose him. Afraid of breaking her promise and disappointing her parents, Amber decided to confide in one of the girls she sang with at school. The older girl she talked with suggested it would be fun to attend prom and have sex on that night because everyone else would be doing it too. As Amber listened, she became afraid of losing out on the chance of going to her boyfriend's prom. She also feared being judged by her girlfriends for remaining a virgin.

Amber, feeling pressured, told Drew she would think about having sex with him on prom night. When prom time came Drew borrowed his favorite aunt's new Corvette to drive to the affair. Amber looked pretty and was dressed in a beautiful, elegant dress. Drew was as sharp as a tack in his tuxedo. Before they got into the Corvette to drive away, Amber's mom whispered a final reminder in her daughter's ear to continue honoring her pledge. Her dad sternly reminded Drew to have Amber home by midnight.

Everyone was enjoying themselves at the dance. The energy was electric, and the deejay played all the hits to make the party live! Just before eleven o'clock Drew suggested they should leave to go and get a motel room. Amber looked around and noticed other couples leaving. She wondered what she should do. She could hear her mother's voice echoing in her head, but Amber could also see her girlfriend signaling her to be brave and leave with Drew. Amber found herself confused, standing frozen in time.

If you were in Amber's shoes, what would you do?

Discussion Questions

- What does it mean to have a spiritual commitment to something like the Pure Flower pledge that Amber is honoring? What are the benefits of honoring such a pledge?

- Have you ever considered taking an abstinence pledge? Why or why not?

- What is the importance of trusting your own judgment and not following what everyone else is doing?

- What would you say to Drew regarding him pressuring Amber to have sex?

- Do you believe Drew really loves Amber? Why or why not? What does true love look like to you?

CHAPTER 5

Untruths & Truths

Most people aspire and attempt to live by root values or personal beliefs which are constructive. However, the unfortunate reality is that because of being miseducated many people live by personal beliefs that are self-destructive and based on falsehood. Personal beliefs which are based on lies represent dysfunctional principles of living and thinking and are known as *untruths*. Personal beliefs that are constructive and which promote healthy living are known as *truths*.

People who live by *un*truths are more likely to misinterpret reality and make decisions based on incorrect information. This may ultimately lead to them becoming trapped in a net of costly negative consequences. To avoid this snare, you need to be aware of some common *untruths* that exist and the *truths* that disprove them. Read the following two lists of Untruths & Truths. As you read each list consider how making a decision might turn out differently based on your acceptance, or rejection, of a given untruth or truth. Living by *truths* will help you become a better person and decision-maker; it will also improve the quality of your relationships with others.

★   ★   ★

YOUNG LADIES' UNTRUTHS & TRUTHS

UNTRUTH – Having physical beauty (hair, nails, make-up, etc.) is most important and should be the sole focus of a young lady's attention.
TRUTH – Physical beauty is nice to have but it is not a young lady's only value. Another kind of beauty is that which comes from within and is shown outwardly in the way you respect yourself and treat others with kindness.

UNTRUTH – A young lady can only be attractive if her body is a certain size, shape, or shade of color.
TRUTH – Young ladies of all sizes, shapes and shades of color are beautiful and worthy of respect and being celebrated. More important than the shape of a young lady's body is the condition of her mind and how she plans to use her ideas to impact the world in a positive way.

UNTRUTH – Having a baby makes you a "grown woman."
TRUTH – Having a baby will certainly make you a mother but it won't make you a woman. Womanhood and motherhood are two different categories. Becoming a woman comes with age and requires demonstrating self-respect, self-discipline and discovering your purpose and living it.

UNTRUTH – A young lady resolves problems by fighting and using violence.
TRUTH – A young lady understands the power of communication and knows how to peacefully resolve disagreements with others without resorting to violence. She does not hit, abuse (verbally or physically), or misuse anyone and realizes everyone is worthy of respect.

UNTRUTH – To be beautiful and attract someone you must dress half-naked.
TRUTH – Most people desire hidden treasures and have great respect for young ladies that do not show or easily give away their goodies.

UNTRUTH – A young lady's worth is determined by how much money or material possessions she has.
TRUTH – Money and material things (clothes, jewelry, cars, etc.) are not a true measurement of a young lady's worth. Your real value lies in your character, spiritual awareness, knowledge, and your willingness to help others.

UNTRUTH – Young ladies cannot perform the same jobs as young men; and even if they do, they don't deserve equal pay.
TRUTH – For the most part, young ladies are fully capable of performing the same jobs as young men and they deserve equal pay for the same work. Young ladies are as smart as young men and should never tolerate being discriminated against because of their gender.

UNTRUTH – Daily prayer is not for young ladies, it is for old people, religious folks, and those in need or in trouble.
TRUTH – Young ladies should seek spiritual enlightenment through prayer, meditation, or some other form of communication with the Higher Power.

UNTRUTH – Young ladies are to be silent when dealing with young men - it is okay for them to be seen but not heard.
TRUTH – Always speak up for yourself and never be silent when wronged or when it's important to express yourself.

UNTRUTH – Going to prison and getting a criminal record is a badge of honor and a sign of toughness.
TRUTH – A smart young lady appreciates her freedom and refuses to participate in behaviors that puts herself and her family at risk of being separated. She understands that going to prison is shameful and causes unimaginable suffering and loss to her entire family and community.

★ ★ ★

YOUNG MEN'S UNTRUTHS & TRUTHS

UNTRUTH – Young men are not supposed to cry, show emotions or be affectionate and empathetic to others.
TRUTH – Young men do cry, and it is good for them to show emotion and verbally express their feelings. They should always be affectionate and empathetic to others because they appreciate the humanity in everyone.

UNTRUTH – A young man resolves problems by fighting and using violence.
TRUTH – A young man understands the power of communication and knows how to peacefully resolve disagreements with others (especially women) without resorting to violence. He does not hit, abuse

(verbally or physically), or misuse any person (woman or man). He realizes that everyone is worthy of respect.

UNTRUTH – For a young man to have an interest in school and strive to become educated he must be a geek or nerd.
TRUTH – Being dumb is for dummies! A young man of purpose seeks knowledge from the cradle to the grave and understands that to be educated is to be empowered!

UNTRUTH – A young man's worth is determined by how much money or material possessions he has.
TRUTH – Money and material things (clothes, jewelry, cars, etc.) are not a true measurement of a young man's worth. Your real value lies in your character, spiritual awareness, knowledge, and your willingness to help others.

UNTRUTH – Young men are naturally smarter than young women.
TRUTH – Both young men and young women alike are smart. The only difference between any two people is their degree of knowledge and experience and how they apply both.

UNTRUTH – Daily prayer is not for young men, it is for old people, religious folks, and those in need or in trouble.
TRUTH – Young men should seek spiritual enlightenment through prayer, meditation, or some other form of communication with the Higher Power.

UNTRUTH – Having sex with lots of young ladies makes you more of a man.
TRUTH – Having sex with lots of young ladies is unhealthy, unwise and has absolutely nothing at all to do with becoming a man.

UNTRUTH – Manhood is determined by the fact that you can make a baby.
TRUTH – Manhood has nothing to do with whether you can produce a baby, but it has much to do with you taking responsibility for the children you create. Real men take care of their children.

UNTRUTH – Disobeying and disrespecting your parents, teachers and other authority figures is a way to prove to others you are grown.
TRUTH – Obeying and respecting your parents, teachers and other authority figures is the proper way to demonstrate you are mature.

UNTRUTH – Going to prison and getting a criminal record is a badge of honor and a sign of toughness.
TRUTH – A smart young man appreciates his freedom and refuses to participate in behaviors that puts himself and his family at risk of being separated. He understands that going to prison is shameful and causes unimaginable suffering and loss to his entire family and community.

Dilemma Tale 1: **Moment of Truth** (Foster Care, Abuse, and Opportunities)

Jordan was fourteen years old and living with his new foster parents, Mr. and Mrs. Green. He had been with them for six months and seemed to like them. They had a nice home, were professional people, and had plenty of time to devote to him since their only adult child lived out of town. The Greens were middle-aged empty-nesters, and they welcomed Jordan with loving arms.

Jordan went into foster care right after his eighth birthday. What would unfortunately become a winding journey through the system all started because his mother was sent to jail for committing a robbery to get money for drugs. His father? Well, Jordan knew very little about his father other than the things he remembered his own mother saying about him. Things like: "You're gonna end up just like your good-for-nothing, broke-ass daddy" and, "Your daddy wasn't nothing more than a sperm donor." Jordan wondered who this "good-for-nothing" man was? What did he look like? What were his interests? And what if his father wasn't exactly as his mother described him, not a "good-for-nothing" after all? Then what would that say about his own value? The big question was why hadn't he been in his son's life? Jordan wondered had he inherited his father's good-for-nothingness? And if so, was this the reason he was in foster care?

Jordan enjoyed staying with Mr. and Mrs. Green, but he wasn't use to things going so well. Having experienced abuse in prior foster care homes made Jordan expect the worst from people. Jordan could remember being repeatedly beaten with an extension cord by a previous foster mother. He remembered living with the Howard family and how they bought nice things for their biological children but refused to buy him anything. The worst abuse Jordan remembered experiencing was the verbal mistreatment he received when living with the Campbell family for two years. Mr. & Mrs. Campbell were a middle-aged husband and wife team with a blended family of six children. They were verbally abusive to their own children as well as to Jordan. Sadly, even the Campbell children became verbally abusive to Jordan. Jordan's foster siblings teased him about his real parents. They constantly told him that he was ugly and made jokes about him being a "foster care failure." Jordan always felt down because to him this kind of abuse was far worse than any physical abuse. The bruises he received from past whippings eventually faded. But the harsh words he heard for so many years remained in his head, playing over and over again like a recording. This was a scar on Jordan's heart, and it caused him to have low self-esteem. He had no expectation that anyone would treat him fairly and with genuine love.

Life was better for Jordan now because he was being exposed to new activities. Mr. Green took him bowling, horseback riding, boating and overnight camping. Jordan really enjoyed these new adventures. However, in the back of his mind Jordan wondered how long it would be before the abuse began. It always seemed to happen the same way in foster homes: good treatment in the beginning only to be followed by mistreatment. Jordan was guarded and began plotting to run away to avoid the Green's becoming cruel to him. He didn't realize it, but the Greens had really taken to him and were beginning to love him like a son. They were great people and genuinely committed to helping him make a life of happiness and success. To finance his runaway trip Jordan came up with the idea to steal Mrs. Green's expensive diamond wedding ring. He figured he'd sell it and get a new start without the Greens. Jordan waited for Mrs. Green to place her ring into her jewelry box. When she finally did, he made his move and stole it.

Mrs. Green soon discovered that her wedding ring was missing. She and Mr. Green were upset and knew that only Jordan could have taken it. Jordan denied any wrongdoing and claimed he was wrongly being accused just so the Greens would have a reason to get rid of him. Mr. Green sat Jordan down for a serious talk. He explained that the ring was special to the family because it was the same ring his mother had received from his father when they married more than sixty years ago. It was a family heirloom intended to be passed down from generation to generation. With tears in his eyes, Mr. Green pleaded with Jordan to return the ring. He promised that all would be forgiven if Jordan gave it back; but if the ring wasn't returned Jordan would have to go. Mr. Green went on to express how much he and his wife were hurt by the theft because they both loved Jordan and viewed him as part of their family. Mr. Green mentioned knowing about the abuse Jordan had experienced and promised he and his wife were only there to help Jordan heal from his troubled past and hoped to adopt him eventually. Jordan was surprised to learn what the ring meant to the Greens, but he was even more shocked to learn they felt so deeply about him. Most of his life he had been told he was worthless, now someone was actually saying he was *worth loving*!

Jordan became torn between holding on to the horrible truth of his painful past experiences and his present want to trust Mr. & Mrs. Green who had showed him nothing but love. He thought about the many good things he and the Greens had done together and how well they had treated him. Jordan also considered the possibility that Mr. Green was trying to trick him into returning the wedding ring only to send him back to the foster care agency. He felt confused. Deep inside he desperately wanted the unconditional love of the Greens, yet the cost of getting it was returning the ring and trusting Mr. Green's promise of forgiveness. This called for Jordan to out himself and face the possibility of being viewed as a thief. But what if telling the truth meant having the opportunity to regain the Greens' trust? Could this be a chance to rebuild their relationship? Jordan stared into space as he remembered the deep pain he often felt when former foster parents promised him love and forgiveness but instead delivered abuse and abandonment.

Jordan wondered if Mr. Green was different than the others, or if he was just the same. Jordan weighed in his mind whether he should exercise faith and trust Mr. Green or rely on his past personal experiences and trust only himself.

If you were in Jordan's shoes, what would you do?

Discussion Questions

- What feelings do you think Jordan experienced when he first went into foster care? Have you or anyone you know ever been in foster care? What was your/their experience like?

- Do you believe Jordan was affected by the negative things he heard about his father? How may it have impacted him? How did the abuse Jordan experienced in foster care affect him? Have you ever been physically and/or verbally abused? If so, what feelings do you have about the abuse and how it has impacted the way you view yourself and life?

- Why do you think Jordan expected Mr. and Mrs. Green to eventually mistreat him? Was his expectation realistic or based on fear?

- How do you think Mr. and Mrs. Green felt when they discovered Jordan stole something very important from them? What feelings do you think Jordan experienced when he learned what the wedding ring really meant to the Green family? How do you think Jordan felt when Mr. Green mentioned that he and his wife loved him and had planned to eventually adopt him?

- Can hurt and pain from your past cause you to reject genuine love and help from people who really care about you? How so? How was Jordan's past experiences of abuse interfering with his present life opportunities? How do you overcome feeling unworthy of being loved to feeling confident and truly worthy of love? Is someone presently trying to help you change your life in a positive way? If so, do you have the courage to accept the help you deserve, or will you allow fear to cause you to run away from it?

Dilemma Tale 2: **Everything Ain't Real** (Social Media, Bullying, and Suicide)

Sixteen-year-old Annette had recently moved to Detroit with her parents. She was excited about attending a new school and looked forward to meeting the cheerleading team because she hoped to earn a spot on the squad. At the start of school Annette attended cheer team tryouts. Most of the girls that showed up were seniors, only a handful were sophomores and juniors. At tryouts Annette noticed a group of girls standing apart from everyone else. One girl appeared to be the leader; she was outspoken and had an imposing presence. Annette heard the other girls refer to her as Kay-Kay, which later she found out were the initials of her name: Kim Karp.

Annette was a junior. She started cheering at just eight years old. She had already been in cheer competitions before and had won a couple of regional titles. Annette had quite a few trophies, but her humble personality never allowed her to brag. During tryouts, the coach questioned Annette about her experience and asked her to perform a solo cheer routine. Everyone seemed impressed with her presentation. The girls flocked to congratulate her as Kay-Kay watched but remained distant. Kay-Kay did not like that her friends were showing interest in the "new girl." Kay-Kay felt she was the only one worthy of being admired since she was popular and pretty. She had been the cheer team's captain the previous year, and now in her senior year she was expecting to lead the squad again.

A couple of weeks later Annette received the exciting news that she had been chosen for the varsity cheerleading squad. Quite naturally Kay-Kay made the team, too. Now it was time for the girls to select their captain. After a team vote it was closely decided that Annette would be the new captain. The girls figured her experience, and leadership would place them in a position of having a shot at winning the regional cheer team competition in the spring. Annette was excited and looked forward to helping her team become better. On the other hand, Kay-Kay wasn't too happy. When she saw her friends Kay-Kay expressed her dissatisfaction about the results of the vote. As the school year went on, her jealousy of Annette grew. She began to think of ways to remove Annette from what she considered was rightfully "her spot."

One night Kay-Kay went on Facebook and posted: "OMG! We have a THOT with HIV at our school! Annette is infected with the virus, check out her HIV/AIDS test results!" Along with this caption Kay-Kay posted a pic of Annette and a fake HIV test result form with Annette's name on it. With the click of her mouse Kay-Kay's many Facebook friends instantly received the post.

For the next few weeks people at school began whispering about the post, and some students even reposted it. The rumor spread like wildfire and before long even students at other schools knew about it. Some students dissed Annette and even refused to sit by her during lunch hour. A few girls on the cheer team no longer liked her and requested that she allow Kay-Kay to be captain. Annette didn't understand why everyone was distancing themselves from her. She started missing classes and regretted her family ever moved to Detroit.

Several weeks later a young man named Drake heard the rumor. Drake was a senior and had lost his favorite aunt to AIDS a year before. He became concerned about Annette when he heard she had HIV; he thought about the emotional and physical hardship Annette was likely experiencing. Drake also noticed many of the other students were shunning Annette, so he decided to befriend her and offer his support. He approached Annette and introduced himself. Happy that someone new was interacting with her, Annette responded kindly and shared her name in return. Drake began with small talk and then began explaining how he had lost his aunt to AIDS. Annette extended her sympathy. Drake thanked her and said, "Annette, I know you just met me, but I would like to offer you my support if you ever need it." Annette asked him what he meant. Drake continued, "Well, it's probably none of my business, but I -I -I, ah....," he stumbled. Annette told him to say what he had to say. Drake continued, "...it's none of my business, but everyone on Facebook says you have HIV and I just want to be your friend and offer my support." "What!", exclaimed Annette. At that moment everything became crystal clear to Annette as to why everyone had been distancing themselves from her. She burst into tears and ran off, leaving Drake standing there, his words hanging in the air.

Annette went home and immediately got on Facebook. She saw her picture and the fake test results along with the many negative comments about her. Totally devastated and angry Annette began sobbing out of control. She thought about how her reputation had been damaged and wondered who would start such a hurtful rumor and why. The more Annette thought about it, the more her mind seemed to focus on Kay-Kay. She knew this was Kim Karp's way of bullying her out of her position on the cheer team. Annette had no idea how to deal with it all. She laid across her bed and couldn't stop crying. Feeling angry and sad, Annette considered taking some pills to end the pain.

If you were in Annette 's shoes, what would you do?

Discussion Questions

- What is cyber-bullying? Have you, or anyone you know, ever been bullied on social media? If so, what happened?

- Is everything that someone puts on social media true? Why or why not? Why did the students at school automatically believe Kay-Kay's post about Annette having HIV?

- What do the letters HIV stand for? What do the letters AIDS stand for? How do you get HIV or AIDS? Do you know anyone that has HIV or AIDS? If so, how is it affecting their life?

- Why do you think Annette considered taking pills?

- Have you, or anyone that you know, ever thought about committing suicide? If you have personally thought about it, did you ever receive help for the issue(s) that bothered you?

- If you or someone you know has thoughts about committing suicide, contact the National Suicide Prevention Lifeline at 1-800-273-8255. The hotline is available 24 hours a day, 7 days a week. Remember, you are not alone.

CHAPTER **6**

Power of No

IT'S YOUR RIGHT

Whenever making an important choice you have the right to say, "No!" No one has the right to force you to do anything, especially something wrong. If a choice doesn't sit well with you, it's both your right and your responsibility to reject it and choose a different path for yourself. Exercise your right to say "No" when you believe a choice will likely produce a negative consequence for you. Becoming a cufflink decision-maker involves learning to recognize and turn down choices that are harmful by firmly saying, "No."

"NO!" GUIDELINES

Cufflink decision-makers generally use one of two sayings to remind themselves to immediately say "No" when faced with an unexpected and important decision-making situation. The pair of sayings are: 1) "It's always better to say "NO" when you do not KNOW", and 2) "If you don't know all of the facts, be smart and step back." In other words, exercise your right to say "No" whenever someone presents you with an important choice you are unsure about. Wait until you gain more knowledge to make an informed decision. Never make serious choices as if life were a video game that you reset once you've crashed and burned from making a critical misjudgment. Some choices once they are made cannot be undone. These etched-in-stone choices sometimes have long-lasting or even lifetime consequences that can be stressful and even painful. Therefore, be sure to stick to the above guidelines whenever presented with a serious decision-making situation that is unclear and has unforeseeable consequences.

IT TAKES COURAGE

What is the shortest word in the English language that very few people want to hear, and many people don't like to say? If the word "No" is your answer you are correct. Many people don't like hearing the word "No," especially if it means their wants or desires are going to go unmet. And many people when asked for something don't feel comfortable telling others "No."

Accepting someone telling you "No" is a big part of growing up and maturing. In life we never get everything we want. However, we do usually get everything we earn. It takes a stable heart and sober mind to receive the word "No" and understand the world hasn't ended simply because you didn't receive what you wanted. The disappointment or rejection you experience from being told "No" can actually be turned into a positive. When you use the experience as motivation for seeking other avenues of achievement it becomes a benefit to you. You can turn lemons into lemonade! Some of the world's greatest success stories are of people who were told "No" but didn't give up on themselves or their dreams.

Practice denying yourself such things as your cellphone or video games for a period of time. This can help you learn to become disciplined and strong where you can accept the word "No" without any problem. Also, fasting for a day or two each month is a great way to experience self-denial and become disciplined. These exercises will strengthen you mentally and emotionally so that you can bear hearing and accepting "No" as an answer. Learning first to accept the word "No" from yourself will certainly make it easier to accept when hearing it from someone else.

★   ★   ★

People who fear saying "No" to others will find themselves quietly and willfully going along with the choices and decisions of others. This is done out of not wanting to appear different or difficult, and it is true among young people and adults alike. However, it is more common with young people because they haven't quite yet discovered the strength of individual identity and, therefore, tend to rely on a shared group identity with their peers. This can be dangerous because anyone who makes an important decision based on the overwhelming influence of someone else does so at the expense of forfeiting the opportunity to make up their own mind. They also risk being held accountable for unimaginable consequences they may not have considered.

It is a challenge to stand up to your peers and say "No" when everyone else in your friend circle is saying "Yes." This personal challenge is about you determining whether it's more important to be yourself and follow your own heart and mind at the risk of being rejected by your peers or whether to follow the suggestions of your peer group at the cost of being untrue to yourself and jeopardizing your dreams and future. A teenager who wants acceptance from a peer group will sometimes disregard his/her own positive voice within. Lacking courage to say "No" and choosing to follow a peer group just for the sake of acceptance is to be dishonest with both yourself and others. Therefore, strive to always be true to yourself by having the courage to say "No" whenever you are not in agreement with a choice or decision someone presents to you. Remember: It's *your* right to say "No!"

SURRENDERING YOUR RIGHT

Under most circumstances you are the only person that can take away your right to say "No". You can surrender this right if you do not speak up for yourself at a time when you should. Failing to speak up while watching someone else make a decision that directly impacts you is a sure way of silently granting them authority to choose for you. An example of this would be to remain silent and stay in the company of a friend that is stealing inside a store. Or, remaining quiet and staying in the back seat of a vehicle as your homies load their weapons and discuss their plan to shoot into someone's house. Not speaking up for yourself in these types of situations is a guaranteed means of granting others the right to dictate choices and circumstances in your life. To remain silent in such a situation is to give up your personal right to responsibly make your own life choices. Surrendering this right can be very costly and could result in you being held accountable for consequences you did not fully consider nor understand at the outset. Giving up your right to say "No" and blindly following someone is a price that is too high to pay just for acceptance. With real friends no cost is involved because you are accepted for who you are and respected for making your own choices. However, *frenemies* do not accept you for who you are. Frenemies pretend to have respect for you so long as you're doing what they want you to do. These so-called friends will also attempt to make you feel guilty when you don't agree with their negative thoughts and schemes. You should never feel guilty for making up your own mind and deciding what is best for yourself. Cufflink decision-makers are smart and know the difference between a friend and a frenemy.

DUI

DUI is commonly defined as "Driving Under the Influence." However, in the cufflink formula world of decision-making the letters are an abbreviation for the term "Deciding Under the Influence." DUI is a personal offense committed against yourself whenever you allow the negative influence of someone to determine your choices. DUIs usually occur when someone feels a need to prove their loyalty and bravado to so-called friends. Such a display of loyalty usually is not based on doing something positive, but rather something negative. Thus, it is important that you recognize and avoid negative influences from other people. A major key to successfully doing this is surrounding yourself with good people that influence you in a positive and helpful manner.

ADVANTAGES OF "NO!"

Have you ever considered what saying "No" could mean for your life? Think about this: Every time you say "No" to skipping class, you indirectly say "Yes" to graduating high school. Every time you say "No" to smoking a blunt, you indirectly say "Yes" to a job opportunity and/or being able to play with your teammates. And when you say "No" to joining a gang, you indirectly say "Yes" to following the rules set by your parents. Every time you say "No" to participating in criminal activity, you indirectly say "Yes" to building a great future for yourself and avoiding prison or an early death. Saying "No" to negative behavior and crime translates into saying "Yes!" to so much more. There is power in the word "No!" Be willing to say "No" to anyone or anything that dims the light of the natural genius within you. Winning in life can be much easier when you understand the true power of "No!"

Dilemma Tale 1: **Hustlin' Homies** (Street-Life Dreams and Drama)

It was mid-summer when the Taylor family moved into their new home. The Johnsons, who lived directly across the street, welcomed them to the neighborhood. It was at this time that Derron Taylor and Collin Johnson first met and became friends. They were both ten years old and neither of them had a father around. Though Derron and Collin somewhat looked alike, they each had a different swagger.

By the time they got to high school both of them had been through a lot. Not only did Derron have to deal with being abandoned by his own father, but he also had to deal with the constant mistreatment from his mother's boyfriend who was also his little sister's dad. This was hard for Derron because it seemed that every man he ever looked up to ended up hurting him. Collin, on the other hand, had to deal with his mother's drinking problem. When his mom wasn't' drinking she was very loving and kind. But if she was drunk, she would act very nasty and curse Collin and say she regretted the day he was born. Whenever Derron's situation at home became unbearable, he would go over to Collin's house. And when Collin's mother was drinking heavily, he would go play video games over at Derron's house in the basement. Derron and Collin talked to one another about their problems and feelings.

At the end of Derron's senior year he ran into Chopper. Chopper was from Derron's old hood and a few years older than him. He was iced-out and driving a steel-grey Chrysler 300. The whip had chrome rims, a Bentley grill, European headlights, tv monitors in the dash and a marching band in the trunk that could be heard bangin' two blocks over. Chopper gave Derron a ride home and told him to call if he ever wanted to start getting some real money. A few days later Derron called Chopper, and for the next year they hustled and made plenty of cash together.

While Derron and Chopper were getting paid with the Get Money Crew, Collin had begun selling drugs with a dude named Fly Guy. Fly Guy was down with the Newbreed Crew and had a reputation for shooting guys whenever he thought they had dissed him. He was known for having a hairpin trigger mentality. He thought that he couldn't be touched by anyone.

Now although Collin and Derron were with different crews, they were still very cool but just didn't hang out together like they used to. They would kick it every now and then when crossing paths in the streets or at a club. But one night when Derron was at home, heated words were exchanged between Chopper and Collin at a local dance club. The argument ended when Collin hit Chopper in the mouth, and a big fight broke out inside the club. The fight spilled outside where Collin then pulled out a burner and fired two shots at Chopper. He missed and Chopper escaped with his life.

The following day Chopper told Derron what happened. Derron was caught off guard by the news. He thought Collin and Chopper were cool with one another, on the basis they both knew they had a mutual friend in him. Chopper then told Derron about having plans to shoot into the house where Collin and his family lived. He said Collin had this coming for attempting to take his life outside the club. Chopper looked Derron in his eyes and said that in a couple of nights they were going to Collin's house to get revenge. He told Derron the only thing he had to do was wait in the car and be the get-away driver. Derron felt a sense of loyalty to Chopper because he had known him since early childhood and for the past year had been with him every day. Derron knew the rules of the game and understood that Collin had broken them. Everyone in the game knows that when something like this occurs there's always a price to pay. Derron was confused since he also felt a strong bond and sense of loyalty to Collin. They had depended on each other many times and were there for one another when neither of their fathers were around. Derron was now caught in the middle of a beef he wished didn't exist.

Derron felt he was being pulled in two different directions, so he shared his feelings with Chopper. In response, Chopper said, "Dawg, I know you are not taking sides with that chump, not after all I've done for you and your fam. I put you on and gave you half of what I got! You knew me long before you knew that lame. We go way back, homie!" Derron stared at the wall and mumbled, "I gotta figure this out, dawg. Both of y'all is my boy, and I don't want to be in the middle of y'all beef. I've ate and slept at my man Collin's house; and you and me are family, no doubt." Chopper, totally uninterested in Derron's point of view, said, "You know the rules of the game! You know how it goes!" Derron responded, "Yeah, I know the rules of the game, but this part ain't mentioned nowhere in the rule book! Damn!" Derron Taylor finds himself at a fork in the road and must decide what to do.

If you were in Derron's shoes, what would you do?

Discussion Questions

- What feelings do you think Derron and Collin experienced from not having a father in their lives? Is your father currently in your life? If not, how do you think his absence affects you?

- How do you think Collin felt about his mother's drinking problem? How did her behavior impact him?

- What are the risks Derron faces by accepting Chopper's invitation to 'get some real paper?'

- What does the "rules of the game" mean to you? Who makes these rules? Are the "rules of the game" good or bad rules and should they be followed?

- Is there a way to work towards peace in this situation? If so, how would you achieve it?

Dilemma Tale 2: **Stand for Something or Fall for Anything** (Peer-Pressure and Personal Choices)

In South Central Los Angeles some of the homeboys and homegirls in the neighborhood would hang out at the Ugly Wall. Originally the Ugly Wall was a nice three-foot-high concrete barrier that framed grass and beautiful flowers growing in front of the apartment building standing directly behind it. But after the riots of the mid-1990s and many years of neglect, the wall was now just a fixture of damaged cinderblocks framing dirt. Every day the youngsters in the 'hood hung out at the Ugly Wall and smoked weed, shot dice, and talked about the drama in their lives.

Late one summer night the homies were hangin' out at the Ugly Wall. One of them suggested they go up the street and break into the Korean-owned neighborhood store. A homie named Fox suggested how it could be done without getting caught. Another homie chimed in that he had the burglary tools to bust the locks. Meanwhile, as everyone else stood around conspiring there was a young man by the name of Trevor who stood silently in the background listening.

Trevor was new in the 'hood and quite different from the thugs he now found himself around. He was from Detroit and had come to L.A. to visit his father for the summer. Trevor hadn't seen his father in almost ten years and never imagined in his wildest dreams he'd be visiting a gang-infested area where crime is the way of life. In Detroit, Trevor had lived with his mother in a plush condo in an upscale community named Sherwood Forest. He had attended private school and earned good grades. Trevor was a charming young man and had promising prospects for a great future should he stay the course. Though he was a decent young man he was now around a bunch of thugs that he likely would be spending the entire summer with. Trevor was unsure of himself and believed the homies' acceptance of him largely depended on whether he went along with their criminal intentions and plots. He felt the need to be someone other than his true self just to get the respect of the homies.

As the fellas stood around waiting for the crew members to return with the burglary tools, Trevor began speaking in a hushed tone. He mumbled something about needing to get home because he had forgotten to do something his father asked of him earlier. The crew was barely able to hear him. Big Melvin then gruffed out, "What da hell you gotta do, lil' homie?" Trevor, afraid to disappoint Big Mel, changed his statement by saying, "Oh, nothing, Big Mel. I said I have something to do whenever we finish." Fat Cat, who was standing next to Big Mel said, "Oh cause' I know you in fresh homie. Hell, you gotta get your feet wet in the game!" Trevor sheepishly nodded his head and in a low voice muttered, "Yeah, I know."

The crew eventually started down the block towards the store. Trevor was shaking on the inside but didn't allow himself to show it. He kept a stern look on his face - a front for those around him. He was very scared and realized what he was doing went against everything his mother taught him. How could he immediately get out of this situation and still be accepted by the gangsta homies? As Trevor continued walking, he thought about lying by saying he had seen a police car. He figured this might make everyone run. But what if it didn't? The thought of his plan failing terrified him as he envisioned receiving a beat down or being labeled a punk for the entire summer. The closer the homies got to the neighborhood store the more Trevor's mind raced. He was running out of time and had to quickly make a decision.

If you were in Trevor's shoes, what would you do?

Discussion Questions

- What does it mean to be accepted by your peers? Have you ever felt pressured to do something you did not feel comfortable doing? Has there ever been a time that you ended up doing something just so that your peers would accept you? How did you feel about your choice after you made it?

- Is it better to stand up for what you believe in or fall for what someone else wants you to do? Why or why not?

- What is peer pressure? How can you recognize it and face it with courage?

- Since Trevor was quite different from the gangbangers he was around, why do you think he felt the need to be accepted by them? Is it better to be yourself or to pretend you are someone you're not?

- Why is it important to be mindful of who you keep company with? Think about this and explain the following two sayings: (1) "If they are not on the way then they're in your way;" and (2) "If you hang around nine broke friends, chances are you'll soon be the tenth."

CHAPTER 7

The Cufflink Formula

LIFE MATHEMATICS

Math was never my favorite subject in school. It took me a little while and a few failing grades before I learned there was an easier way to solve math problems. After falling behind in algebra class, one day my teacher spoke six magical words to me. She pulled me aside after class and said, "You need to learn the formula." Upon hearing this great advice, a light instantly came on in my head. At that very moment I became aware that for every math problem there is a formula to solve it. This meant that if I could learn various formulas, I would be able to figure out the correct answer to any math problem. My teacher's advice was truly eye-opening! Soon after learning the formula for algebra, I noticed an improvement in my grades. My self-confidence soared when I no longer had to struggle and guess the answers. I felt good about myself when I gained an understanding of how to solve math problems.

Life is very similar to math class because we are always confronted with problems to solve. And just like with math problems, our life problems can be solved by using the correct formula. When addressing problems in life you either use a correct problem-solving formula or a wrong one. Using an incorrect formula to solve a life problem will likely result in the wrong answer. Whereas using a correct problem-solving formula will help you get the right answers/solutions to your life problems. Wouldn't it be cool to learn a method (formula) that helps you always come away with the right answer? This would help you avoid many mistakes and also likely save you lots of heartache.

IS YOUR FORMULA WORKING?

In this chapter you will learn how to solve life problems using the Cufflink Formula. Before we introduce you to the formula, let's first look at the formula (method) which you currently use to make decisions. Think of the last serious problem or dilemma you had and list in order what steps you took to solve it (make the list as long as needed). Okay. What does your list reflect? Was it difficult to recall and list in order the steps you took? If you are anything like me when I was a teenager, then you've probably never given serious thought about the way in which you solve problems or make decisions -- it's just something you do without effort. It's simple. You find yourself facing a set of choices or having a problem to deal with and you just make a decision. Case closed. Nothing to talk about, right? WRONG!!! Was the problem solved? Could you have gotten a better outcome had you done more research or given the situation more thought? Did your decision/choice affect you or others in a negative way? Was there something you forgot to consider? Did anything unexpected happen? Did you misjudge or underestimate anything or anyone? And was your decision based on how you felt at the time? These are questions to consider when trying to understand the effectiveness of the problem-solving formula you use. If you are fed up with using a method (formula) that often produces negative consequences and leaves you dissatisfied, then the Cufflink Formula is exactly what you need.

WHAT IS THE CUFFLINK FORMULA C=vcd²?

C stands for Consequences; *v* for root values, the deeply held personal beliefs each person has; *c* for choices available; and *d²* stands for the four-step decisioning process required to make an informed decision. The Cufflink Formula, *C=vcd²*, therefore, is based on the premise that consequences themselves are determined by your root values and available choices multiplied by the quality of your decisioning squared. The complete process involves Framing, Choice Searching, Values Alignment Check, Decisioning Squared, and Making the Cufflink Decision (see The Cufflink Formula Worksheet).

FRAMING

Framing is a two-step process that involves Decoding and Gauging. This two-step process can be very helpful in putting problems and dilemmas in the correct perspective so they can be solved right. Decoding is properly defining a problem to increase the likelihood of making a cufflink decision rather than a regretful handcuff decision. Gauging is measuring your emotional connection to a problem or dilemma and setting aside whatever feelings you must to get a rational and balanced perspective (framing) of the issue(s) involved. Properly framing a problem is critical to the problem-solving process because it affects how the problem is viewed and subsequently resolved by the decision-maker. When our framing is on point, we are more likely to respond to problems in a healthy and productive manner. However, when our framing is faulty or based on misinformation, we are more apt to respond to problems in an unproductive way. Framing is important because the goal of problem-solving is to always get the best result consistent with your highest values and healthiest aspirations!

Decoding

People in groups often have a particular language designed to help them communicate more effectively among themselves. This happens within small and large groups and in both the professional world and the streets. There are different forms of language (standard English, slang, street lingo, jargon, etc.), yet slang and street lingo appear to have a major influence on today's youth. Slang and street lingo are commonly used in rap songs, music videos and across social media.

Perhaps what seems cool about slang is that it allows people to present broad concepts, thoughts and feelings in a few simple words. In other words, we can use shortened forms of language to verbally express our ideas and emotions without presenting every detail. Although this might be convenient, it can also be a serious disadvantage when used in decision-making and problem-solving. The disadvantage is that important information is often lost in translation and therefore never considered. On the surface coded messages of slang and street lingo sound slick, harmless and enticing. However, beneath the surface of each slick term is the true meaning of a broader expression or idea. Therefore, while it is important to pay attention to what's being said, it is equally important you pay even more attention to what's not being said. Consider these few examples of slang that have each been decoded:

Coded Slang – Let's hit a lick; or let's finesse that guy.
Decoded – Let's violate someone by STEALING their property.

Coded Slang – Forget school, I'm going to hustle in a trap house.
Decoded – I'm going to SKIP SCHOOL and sit in a DRUG HOUSE to illegally make money.

Coded Slang – We're gonna run bustos (a train) on that hood rat.
Decoded – We are going to totally DISRESPECT and VIOLATE someone's sister, daughter, or mother by RAPING and GANG SEXING her.

Coded Slang – I'm going to put some holes in him.
Decoded – I'm going to SHOOT someone and DESTROY THEIR LIFE AND MY OWN.

Coded Slang – She's hating on me.
Decoded – She simply doesn't AGREE WITH ME and THINKS FOR HERSELF.

Coded Slang – He's a hoe and I don't like him.
Decoded – He is DIFFERENT and DETERMINED and I'm probably jealous of him.

Slang and street lingo can easily distort the true meaning of a situation, choice, or problem by describing it as something other than what it actually is. The result can be that serious matters are taken lightly and not treated with respectful consideration for their consequences, while trivial matters might be overreacted to and taken way too seriously. Be sure to always pull back the curtain of coded language so that you see the bare truth regarding a choice or problem. Your ability to survive and make cufflink decisions largely depends on how well you can avoid the language traps associated with slang and street lingo.

Decoding is all about peeling away the smooth covering of coded language from the real issue to be considered. It allows for proper framing and an informed decision to be made by the decision-maker. To do this, get into the habit of rewording (translating) coded language into plain terms. This will enhance your understanding, deepen your insight, and help you put problems and dilemmas in the correct perspective. As a cufflink problem-solver you should always take the time to decode each coded message into plain language to understand its true meaning.

Gauging

Framing also requires you to truthfully gauge your emotional connection to a problem or choice. To do this you must be aware of your feelings. Some emotions people commonly experience when dealing with problems and choices can include excitement, anger, fear, anxiety, hope, loneliness, jealousy, envy, and love. To some degree or another, we all experience one or more of these kinds of emotions when confronted with problems and choices. However, to really understand your emotional connection to a specific problem or choice calls for you to pause and reflect on how you really feel regarding the matter. Identify your feelings and determine whether your emotional state already existed or was sparked by the problem or choice you presently face. Making such a determination grants you an opportunity to recognize the degree of influence your emotions have on your thought process.

Feelings are personal and can sometimes be intense. Left unchecked, our feelings (emotions) can cause us to incorrectly frame problems and choices. Viewing problems through an emotional lens is risky because it causes misjudgments that can lead to negative consequences. Failure to get hold of your emotions and not using your head to think through a situation can result in disastrous and regretful consequences. Allowing your emotions (anger, excitement, fear, loneliness, etc.) to be the reason for a decision does not guarantee that later you will feel the same way about the matter you decided. In fact, the more your emotions influence the framing process and your decision the more likely it is that your feelings will change later. Think about it. No one remains angry, sad, happy, or indifferent forever. Therefore, it is important to put your feelings in correct perspective when confronted with a serious problem or choice. This helps you make a clear, unbiased, and thoughtful determination about the problem and what choice you should make. Gauging your emotions is an important step in the problem-solving process and therefore it needs to be on point. Be mindful and PAUSE whenever your emotions are running high, then address the problem later when you are calm.

CHOICE SEARCHING

You have framed your problem or dilemma, but how will you address it? In other words, "What choice will you make?" Wait! Never be too quick to go with the first thing that comes to mind, it could be the wrong choice! Instead, take your time and engage in choice searching. This is the process of using your creative mind to think of various options you will consider and can test before making a final choice. Choice searching is about expanding your thought process and thinking outside the box when resolving problems or dilemmas. One great way to expand your selection of options is to seek the advice of your parents, pastor, teachers, or mentor(s). You might be surprised by the suggested options you receive from people that have previous experience with the same kind of problem or dilemma you seek to resolve. Tapping into the wisdom and insight of others can help you identify great options you may not have otherwise considered. Choice searching also requires you to consider options that are unpopular or culturally unfamiliar. After you identify your options, you can list each one in an individual option box under the "Choices" column in the worksheet.

VALUES ALIGNMENT CHECK

Now that you've come up with a list of options you will need to conduct a values alignment check on each of them. A values alignment check is for determining how each individual option sits in relation to your positive root values (belief system). You must decide if the option should be: (1) accepted as a possible choice; (2) cautiously considered as a possible choice; or, (3) rejected.

If you decide that an individual option aligns with your values (beliefs), place a check (✓) next to "Yes" in the adjacent box. The check means you have given the option (potential choice) strong recommendation for consideration. Or, if you determine an option is values-neutral (i.e., it doesn't offend your moral and spiritual beliefs) you should then place a check (✓) next to 'Neutral'. A check here means that you will cautiously consider the option as a possible final choice. And, if you determine an option contradicts or offends your positive root values and morals, simply place a check (✓) next to "No." A check here signifies you have dismissed the option altogether from consideration. Each option can only receive a single rating.

A values alignment check serves the important purpose of making sure the choices you ultimately consider are based on your root values. Values-based choices have to do with what is morally right and fair. Considering important choices that are values-based related makes it easier to reject choices that are negative and don't square with your personal values. Rejecting choices that conflict with your positive values is a great way to practice integrity and helps you feel good about yourself. You should never make a choice that compromises your positive root values, nor should you make one that makes you feel bad.

Your outright rejection of an offensive choice does not mean you lack understanding of its likely consequences; it just means that because the choice conflicts with your values it becomes unnecessary to waste time exploring its potential outcome. When you stand by your positive root values the attraction of instant gratification is not enough to make you compromise your moral and spiritual principles. Your moral and spiritual principles are an anchor which prevents you from drifting into the sea of mischief and trouble. Life can become very complicated when you get away from your base of positive values. Be sure to remain true to your values and stay anchored in positive thoughts and good behavior.

DECISIONING SQUARED

The options that you determine are in agreement with your positive root values and the ones you determine are values-neutral must now be tested in theory. This is done by using critical thinking to examine the *how*, *why*, *what if* and *reasonableness* of each option before accepting or acting on any one of them. Rather than impulsively making a decision because a particular choice sounds good or delivers immediate pleasure, decisioning squared requires you thoroughly test each option by: (1) weighing its pros & cons; (2) determining best & worst-case scenarios; (3) evaluating your true feelings; and (4) assessing its trait identities. Subjecting each option upfront to this type of critical review will provide a clear understanding of both the obvious and hidden factors of a potential choice.

Critical Thinking

Successful decision-making using critical thinking requires you to be in the disciplined habit of narrowing your focus for each option. This calls for asking yourself probing questions that do more than scratch the surface of common curiosity. Critical thinking is about being open to new information and fresh ideas even if the information and ideas are unfamiliar or contradict what you believe to be true. Critical thinking not only means asking questions but being willing to change your mind in the face of new and credible facts. As a critical thinker you should resist being closed-minded or blinded by your opinions and feelings. Seek out the facts (truth) by asking piercing questions that burst into inflated or biased opinions and reward you with detailed information that is useful in making an informed decision. Look for contradictions, too. Identifying them will help dispel false notions and misconceptions that often lead to handcuff decisions. Be a wise cufflink decision-maker by applying critical thinking to your decision-making.

Pros & Cons

What are pros & cons? Simply put, pros are arguments in favor of something; cons are arguments against something. Whether you are on the debate team or just want to be a cufflink decision-maker, pros & cons are helpful tools for ensuring that both sides of an issue or choice are clearly seen. Having knowledge of pros & cons can really improve your decision-making and problem-solving ability. Understanding both sides of a situation can grant you massive insight about the risks and rewards associated with each choice. This in turn will help you pre-determine if a choice is worth the investment of your time and energy. Your life is your million-dollar business, and you alone are Chief Executive Officer! As CEO your job is to invest in positive choices that lead to the fulfillment of your dreams and life purpose. Each important choice you make should be well-thought out, decisive, and helpful to you being your best self.

To make a pros & cons comparison list, use your critical thinking skills to think of the plain, and not so obvious reasons why a particular choice would be good or bad. List those reasons side-by-side on a sheet of paper or in the pros & cons columns of The Cufflink Formula Worksheet (see worksheet at the end of this chapter). A side-by-side listing removes any guesswork and helps you mentally weigh the benefits and disadvantages of each choice. As you consider the pros & cons, be more mindful of the quality rather than the quantity of your reasons. Although one column's listing may be longer than the other, it doesn't necessarily mean that based on that factor alone a choice should be outright followed or rejected. The pros & cons comparison is the initial step of the decision-making process. As you read on, you'll see there are other steps to the process that must be completed to arrive at a balanced cufflink decision.

Best & Worst-Case Scenarios

When reviewing the options from which you'll make a choice, be sure to consider what the best- & worst-case scenarios are for each. Prefiguring the best & worst-case scenarios that can occur with a choice gives you great advantages. One advantage is being able to predetermine how you will feel if things were to turn out ideally or drastically. If you find that the best-case scenario wouldn't quite meet your expectations, or the worst-case scenario would be too drastic for you to bear, knowing this beforehand could be enough to persuade you to dismiss an option and consider another in its place. Contemplating best- & worst-case scenarios gives you an edge by minimizing or eliminating altogether your chances of being surprised by unforeseeable outcomes. Reducing the surprise element involves being thoughtful, deliberate, and farsighted in your decision making.

Thinking about best & worst-case scenarios can also help you understand the range of influence and impact a choice may have on other people. You should practice empathy by considering how your choice will affect others.

True Feelings

Having already completed your values alignment check, pros & cons, and best-& worst-case scenarios analysis, you are now ready to check what your true feelings are regarding each choice option. Begin by reviewing all the information you've gathered about Option 1. Relax and consult your heart about how this option makes you feel. Think about how you would truly feel if this option were your only choice. How would its likely consequences make you feel? Indifferent (uncertain/confused), happy, excited, disappointed, or possibly angry? Determine your true feelings for Option 1, and repeat this same process with Option 2, Option 3, etc.

Cufflink Formula True Feelings Diagram

Note: These five categories of human emotion represent the basic range of feelings typically experienced in decision-making & problem-solving situations.

Honestly answering how each option makes you feel is important to the decisioning process. Why? Because however you feel about your final choice will likely be reflected in your behavior and the way your decision is carried out. Be mindful of your feelings and take them seriously as you go through the decisioning process. It's you that will have to live with the results of each decision you make, so consult your heart and be honest about your true feelings.

Traits

The Cufflink Formula model suggests that every authoritative choice has four basic qualities. These basic qualities known as traits are what gives each option/choice its identity and allows it to be accurately defined.

The four trait categories from which an authoritative choice gains its identity are:

- Rational   or - Emotional   or - Intuitive
- Self-serving   or - People-Serving (Selfless)
- Value-based   or - Peer-based
- Reversible   or - Permanent

Rational, Emotional, or Intuitive

A rational choice is one that is well thought-out and has been rigorously tested for reasonableness. The process for making a rational choice involves using the rational mind for gathering information about an option, weighing its benefits and disadvantages, analyzing the "what ifs" of both sides, then and comparing it to other options and deliberating its outcome to determine how it will ultimately make you feel. If a majority of all criteria have been satisfied the option turned final choice has a rational trait identity.

An emotional choice is made based on a person's present emotional charge or state. Because the emotional mind tends to cloud judgment, it is these decisions (choices) which are usually carried out impulsively and with little concern for the outcome. This can leave the decision-maker vulnerable to unforeseeable and harsh consequences that are long-term. Choices made based on emotions are typically a direct result of someone either: (1) refusing altogether to think options through and subject them to a test of reasonableness; or (2) totally disregarding critical information even after subjecting options to a test of reasonableness. Either way, emotions rather than rationale become the main influence in the decision-making process. When emotions are the dominant theme the option/choice has an emotional trait identity.

An intuitive choice is based on having a strong gut feeling about a particular choice without knowing all the facts. The wisdom from a person's awareness, experience and spirituality are the guiding forces behind these types of choices, not present logical thought processes. Intuitive choices therefore are trust-based decisions that come from a strong inner-conviction and desire for achieving the best outcome. A choice that has the above qualities has an intuitive trait identity.

Self-serving or People-serving

A self-serving choice aims to fulfill one's interests and personal needs. Based foremost on the lofty principle of loyalty to self, self-serving choices focus on accomplishing the positive aspirations and goals of the decision-maker. Self-serving choices are integrity-based and shouldn't be confused with selfishness; whereby personal agendas are met at the expense of stepping on others. Choices which bring out the best in you are defined as self-serving, while choices that diminish your personhood are considered self-defeating. Any choice which places your positive interests in the forefront has a self-serving trait identity.

A people-serving (selfless) choice is typically made from a spirit of kindness. It comes from a personal desire to assist in the fulfillment of someone else. At its core, a people-serving choice is based on the principle of self-sacrifice. Generally, it involves the noble act of denying oneself for the benefit of another.

Any option or choice requiring self-sacrifice and that puts the interests of others first has a people-serving trait identity.

Values-based or Peer-based

Values-based choices are an extension of the decision-maker's moral and spiritual commitments (root values). They present the opportunity for personal beliefs to be demonstrated through action. Making values-based choices requires having root values as your guiding principle. This calls for resisting the urge to give into the temptation of making choices just because they may be popular or convenient. Values-based choices ensure that the decision-maker maintains his/her moral footing and feels confident about their choice. When root values are the basis for a decision the choice has a values-based trait identity.

Peer-based choices are based on influences from friends or peers. These types of choices are usually the result of a decision-maker's willingness to abandon their own thinking. The intense fear of rejection and the desire for acceptance by others can sometimes cause a youth to make a bad choice. Young people, you are on a sacred journey of initiation. The journey includes the experience of self-discovery and understanding how you fit in with friends, peers, and the larger world. Sometimes fear of rejection and the desire to fit in can seem stronger than the need for self-discovery and self-expression. When this happens, you can become vulnerable to falling under the influence of others and trying to live up to their expectations. It is because of this risk that all peer-based choices must be thoroughly examined. However, it must be noted that not all peer-based choices are negative. There are many situations in which the influence of friends and peers can be positive. This is especially true when friends are there to encourage you to be positive and do what's right when you may be thinking of doing something wrong. Any choice that is based on the influence of friends or peers has a peer-based trait identity.

Reversible or Permanent

A reversible choice is a changeable decision. Once it is made it can later be modified, abandoned, or replaced with another choice that provides a different outcome. This type of choice provides flexibility because of the opportunity to undo it. A good example of a reversible choice would be deciding to transfer from a university in another state to a college in your home state. Having gone to school out-of-state for a year, you realize you don't like being away from family, so you change your educational plan. Another good example is quitting an after-school job because you notice a decline in your grades and therefore need more study time. Any choice that can be undone and which doesn't have permanent consequences has a reversible trait identity.

A permanent choice is a decision that cannot be changed once made. The permanence of the choice lies in its unchangeable consequences which usually have far-reaching effects. An example of this would be someone making the decision to have sex for the first time. Once it is performed, a sexual encounter cannot be undone and the risks of pregnancy and/or contraction of an STI (sexually transmitted infection) cannot be avoided. Another good example is being uptight for cash and deciding to commit a robbery to get money. Once a crime is committed, it cannot be undone; no matter how much a person may regret it. Crime produces serious and permanent consequences such as a lifetime victim, criminal record, incarceration and karma. Authoritative choice decisions that are permanent in nature should only be made after making a thorough cufflink evaluation and giving serious consideration to consequences. Any choice that has longstanding, irreversible consequences have a permanent trait identity.

Having knowledge of the traits associated with each option provides you valuable information and helps you see the bigger picture. It also provides you a clear understanding about how each potential choice will likely impact yourself and others.

MAKING THE CUFFLINK DECISION

It is now time to make a determination as to which options are the two topmost you want to consider for your final choice. This means conducting a brief review of all that you've learned about each option and then deciding which two best represent who you are. Write down these two choices on The Cufflink Formula Worksheet.

Next, consult your heart and decide which option best accomplishes your overall objective and will be your final choice. You can meditate or pray about the decision if you believe this will be helpful. Whatever you do, please don't procrastinate or begin over-thinking because these impostors are the enemies of cufflink decision-making. Be confident and make the choice you believe is best.

To complete your knowledge of the Cufflink Formula you must be aware of the one exception to decision-making. It is: "No matter how much you may analyze your final choice there is always the possibility for things to turn out other than how you planned." Prepare for this possibility by devising a back-up plan and writing it down on the worksheet. Having a back-up plan will make you feel even more secure in your decision-making.

Now that you've learned the Cufflink Formula you should feel confident in your ability to solve any problem or dilemma. This newfound confidence should translate into making great decisions that improve the quality of your life and the lives of those around you. Cufflink decision-making is an art! Regularly using the Cufflink Formula will help you master the process. Put your new knowledge into practice and begin being proud of each cufflink decision you make. Congratulations!

CUFFLINK FORMULA™ WORKSHEET

FRAME: Problem/ Dilemma

CHOICES	VALUES ALIGNMENT ✓	PROS ⊕	CONS ⊖	BEST CASE SCENARIO	WORST CASE SCENARIO	TRUE FEELINGS	TRAITS
Option 1	— No (STOP) ● — Neutral (CAUTION) ○ — Yes (PROCEED) ●	1) 2) 3)	1) 2) 3)	OUTCOME	OUTCOME	Select One	Emotional/Rational/Intuitive Self-serving/ People-serving Value-based/ Peer-based Reversible/ Permanent
Option 2	— No (STOP) ● — Neutral (CAUTION) ○ — Yes (PROCEED) ●	1) 2) 3)	1) 2) 3)	OUTCOME	OUTCOME	Select One	Emotional/Rational/Intuitive Self-serving/ People-serving Value-based/ Peer-based Reversible/ Permanent
Option 3	— No (STOP) ● — Neutral (CAUTION) ○ — Yes (PROCEED) ●	1) 2) 3)	1) 2) 3)	OUTCOME	OUTCOME	Select One	Emotional/Rational/Intuitive Self-serving/ People-serving Value-based/ Peer-based Reversible/ Permanent
Option 4	— No (STOP) ● — Neutral (CAUTION) ○ — Yes (PROCEED) ●	1) 2) 3)	1) 2) 3)	OUTCOME	OUTCOME	Select One	Emotional/Rational/Intuitive Self-serving/ People-serving Value-based/ Peer-based Reversible/ Permanent
Option 5	— No (STOP) ● — Neutral (CAUTION) ○ — Yes (PROCEED) ●	1) 2) 3)	1) 2) 3)	OUTCOME	OUTCOME	Select One	Emotional/Rational/Intuitive Self-serving/ People-serving Value-based/ Peer-based Reversible/ Permanent

TRUE FEELINGS: Angry / Disappointed / Indifferent / Happy / Excited

Top Two Choices: 1.   2.

Final Decision

Back-up Plan

Worksheet Instructions

1. Frame and clearly define your problem/ dilemma.
2. List your different options.
3. Determine whether or not each option aligns with your root values.
4. Use critical thinking to determine the pros and cons.
5. Write down the best and worst case scenarios.
6. Review your true feelings by determining how you would feel having a particular option as a final choice.
7. Consider the basis of each option and determine its traits.
8. Weigh all info you've gathered, then decide which are your top two choices.
9. Decide, then write down your final choice/ decision.
10. Decide, then write down your back-up plan.

CUFFLINK FORMULA™ PLEDGE

I Pledge

I [Your Name], pledge to honor myself by adopting positive root values that promote healthy thinking and good behavior.

I pledge to be in charge of and accountable for my words and actions.

I pledge to think for myself and make my own decisions rather than allowing others to think and decide for me.

I pledge to seek more knowledge and options and weigh the pros and cons of important choices before committing to any course of action.

I pledge to make a choice only after considering how its consequences will impact me, my family and community.

I pledge to make choices which are good and that do not aim to misuse, offend or hurt others.

Finally, I pledge to be responsible for myself by making positive decisions that lead to my success and happiness in life!

I Am A Cufflink Decision-Maker!
I Choose CUFFLINKS over Handcuffs!

AFTERWORD

In 2007, myself and a few other incarcerated men at Ryan Correctional Facility (now the Detroit Reentry Center) came together to discuss how we could help address the problem of the "schoolyard to prison-yard pipeline" that funnels underprivileged children from classrooms into prison cells. We realized that with each passing year the prison population was becoming younger. This was a sign of the continued destruction of family and community structures, a catastrophic phenomenon which we were regretful for having played a part through some of our past choices. From behind prison walls, we decided to do something that could help repair our community. Our collective effort resulted in committing ourselves to do everything we can to save as many young lives as possible.

This joint commitment inspired us to start the new Youth Deterrent Program (the original program was started at Ryan by former prisoner Stan Nelson and ran during 1992-1994). Our basic aim was to deter young boys from engaging in criminal thinking and behavior. We figured that by sharing our life stories, we would demystify for young boys the life-and-death dance of making positive choices. Our deterrent model would be based on a "Cared Straight" approach. This meant that we would appeal to the intelligence and moral consciousness of the youth rather than rely on intimidation tactics. We understood the new Youth Deterrent Program (YDP) would need to harness community resources to help heal the issues the youth revealed during the sessions, so we began building supportive partnerships with various organizations and agencies within the community.

To prepare us for the important work of mentoring youth, we received training in Choice Theory, Reality Therapy, and Story Therapy from Bishop Mbiyu Chui of the Shrine of the Black Madonna. Training in Levels of Response to Traumatic Events (a tool for children of incarcerated parents, created by Joyce Dixon, MSW) was taught to us by Dr. Carl Taylor of Michigan State University. We also received training from Thomas J. Adams and Jessica Taylor of the Chance for Life Organization; they taught us critical thinking, diversity, communication skills, ethical reasoning, basic cognitive restructuring and mediation.

For more than eleven years we have used these tools to mentor more than three thousand male youth. Additionally, for the past three years under the leadership of Parole Agent Verlynda Winston we've mentored over three hundred young adult probationers in the Wayne County Residential Alternative to Prison (WRAP) program inside the Detroit Reentry Center. Mentoring both justice-involved youth and young probationers accorded us the opportunity to notice a common pattern in their approach to decision-making. That pattern can best be described as "impulsive, absent the benefit of forethought", and it is the same "handcuff formula" most of us had used when we were impressionable young men. Reflecting on some of the bad choices I made in the past compelled me to think how my actions hurt others and myself. This reflection brought on a strong desire within me to do something significant to help prevent young people from making bad choices and possibly losing their young lives to prison or death. I believed that if young people were taught an effective way of approaching decision-making it would likely prevent them from victimizing others and help save their own lives.

Participating in our monthly YDP sessions were fulfilling. However, I saw the need to expand the healing process beyond the prison visiting room where our transformative sessions are held. Our youth need to be educated on how to make good choices. To bring this knowledge to more young people I committed to writing this book.

Writing *The Cufflink Formula* was always more than just a literary project; it is an expression of my life's purpose. It required putting my love, creativity, and humanity onto every page for the sake of helping justice-involved youths reclaim their natural genius. In reclaiming the best of themselves young people will be able to identify and share their inner gifts with the world. I am prayerful this book will be helpful in achieving this important objective.

I hope *The Cufflink Formula – A Young Person's Guide To Decision-Making* has served you well and enhanced your ability to make great decisions! May You Be blessed!

Everett Rocklin Jackson

ABOUT THE AUTHOR

[Everett] Rocklin Jackson was twenty-one years of age when he was convicted of murder and sentenced to Life in 1987. Upon entering prison, he was fortunate to meet many dedicated prison volunteers who encouraged him to invest in his academic and spiritual growth. Rocklin began attending all classes and programs offered in prison and these were the first steps in his journey of transformation.

Through a divine act of grace Rocklin Jackson was introduced to mentors Tom Adams and Jessica Taylor of the Chance for Life Organization (CFL). He is a core member of CFL and has honed his leadership and mediation skills under the tutelage of these inspiring mentors. As a mediator he has helped reduce the number of violent incidences in prison by conducting mediations between other prisoners.

Rocklin Jackson heads the NAACP Prison Program Committee and facilitates the Youth Deterrent Program inside the Detroit Reentry Center (DRC). He is a "Teaching Assistant" for the Inside/Out College Program sponsored through Wayne State University. Rocklin recently created the Poetry Workshop Series, a ten-week poetry course for prisoners hosted by poets from the metropolitan-Detroit area. Dedicated to helping young people turn their lives around, Rocklin Jackson mentors probationers at DRC using his signature style teaching in the classroom to impart the valuable lessons of *The Cufflink Formula.*

Incarcerated more than three decades Rocklin Jackson has evolved into a writer, performer of poetry, teacher, and is a motivational speaker. He spends his time writing, studying, creating educational programs, and mentoring young people.

www.ingramcontent.com/pod-product-compliance
Lightning Source LLC
Chambersburg PA
CBHW062051090426
42740CB00016B/3099

* 9 7 8 0 5 7 8 5 4 5 2 8 8 *